Come and Sit

Other books in the
A Week Inside Series

Making a Heart for God: A Week Inside a Catholic Monastery
Waking Up: A Week Inside a Zen Monastery

Come and Sit

A Week Inside Meditation Centers

Marcia Z. Nelson

Foreword by Wayne Teasdale

Walking Together, Finding the Way

SKYLIGHT PATHS PUBLISHING

Come and Sit:
A Week Inside Meditation Centers

© 2001 by Marcia Z. Nelson

For information regarding permission to reprint material from this book, please mail or fax your request in writing to SkyLight Paths Publishing, Permissions Department, at the address / fax number listed below.

Library of Congress Cataloging-in-Publication Data
Nelson, Marcia Z.
    Come and sit : a week inside meditations centers / Marcia Z. Nelson ;
      foreword by Wayne Teasdale.
          p.   cm.
      Includes bibliographical references.
      ISBN 1-893361-35-7 (pbk.)
      ISBN-13: 978-1-68336-553-2 (pbk)
      1. Meditation. I. Title.
    BL627 .N45 2001
    291.4'35—dc21   2001005446

Manufactured in the United States of America

SkyLight Paths, "Walking Together, Finding the Way" and colophon are trademarks of LongHill Partners, Inc., registered in the U.S. Patent and Trademark Office.

Walking Together, Finding the Way
Published by SkyLight Paths Publishing
An Imprint of Turner Publishing Company
4507 Charlotte Avenue, Suite 100
Nashville, TN 37209
Tel: (615) 255-2665
www.skylightpaths.com

For Bill, the light of my path

Contents

Foreword

There is considerable evidence everywhere we look that we have entered a new age—not in the sense of the "New Age movement," but in the sense of a radically novel period of history. Bede Griffiths, the English Benedictine monk, writer, and spiritual teacher who went to India in 1955 to "seek the other half of my soul," as he put it to a friend at the time, often spoke of the new age we were rapidly entering. This new age can be characterized as essentially *interspiritual,* since it measures the breakdown of barriers separating the religions as more and more people cross boundaries to explore the treasures of the various traditions. The Interspiritual Age is one in which people are interested more in mystical spirituality, and less in religion. Mysticism is direct awareness and experience of Ultimate Reality, the Divine Mystery, God, or the Infinite Spirit. It is the commitment to a mystical, experiential path that sets off the Interspiritual Age from all other ages.

Everywhere I go, I meet people who have awakened or are awakening to the mystical path, who have embraced a disciplined form of spirituality, and who have taken responsibility for their own development and refuse to leave it to an institution such as their church, synagogue, temple, or mosque. My students are no exception; they seem bored with religion, but vitally fascinated with spirituality. Please don't misunderstand: I'm not trying to disparage the role and value of religion. It is important and needed, and it is an integral component of human culture and historical experience. The religions will always exist; they are repositories of vast experience, insight, and methodology. We stand on the shoulders of these great traditions, and of the giants who produced them and nourished their development over the centuries.

This is as it should be, since all the great world religions arose from the mystical processes of their founders. The Hindu tradition, the *Sanatana Dharma*, the Eternal Religion, came into being through the mystical experiences of the *rishi*s, the forest sages of ancient India. The dharma of the Buddhist culture has its origin in the inner awakening of Gautama Siddhartha Sakyamuni, the Buddha, the Enlightened One. His enlightenment experience is paradigmatic for all Buddhists. Similarly, the Jewish tradition owes its existence to the patriarchs and prophets of ancient Israel, who all encountered God, or Yahweh. Their encounters became the basis of their mandate for prophecy, giving them the courage to speak in God's name. Christianity sprang from the inner consciousness of Jesus, who was intensely aware of his intimate relationship with the mysterious One he called his Father. The Prophet Muhammad received a private revelation from Allah through the mediation of the archangel Gabriel. In each case, these traditions were born in mysticism and developed through a historical unfolding of tradition, which attempted to transmit the means of transformation.

Mystical spirituality requires some sort of contemplative method of prayer or meditation, and these methods become the way to break through to the other side, to part the veil in order to see where everything comes from, and to where it will all return. They are ways to deepen our knowledge of reality, others, God, and ourselves. They are roads to explore the inner life of the spiritual journey, the mystical quest for the Absolute, as Hindus would have it.

Mysticism, or mystical spirituality, existed long before any of the religions, the oldest of which is not more than seven thousand years old. Mysticism may be as old as fifty to one hundred thousand years. Both yoga and meditation are extremely ancient, even timeless, in their origin. The religions are attempts to institutionalize and thereby hold on to the moment of mystical realization. It seems only natural and appropriate that the religions would return to their roots in mysticism and spirituality, that they would be renewed and refreshed in their common source. In a very real sense, the great religions exist not as ends in themselves, but as different means to reach the same goal: transformation of consciousness, will, memory, imagination, and, most important, the heart. Each tradition possesses a direction to ultimate consciousness, methods to arrive there, and countless guides to the way.

The goal in each tradition of spirituality is differently conceived, depending on the historical experience and the influence of this experience on its founder or founders. There are roughly three possibilities, or three models, of spiritual development, and they can be outlined as the Hindu, the Buddhist, and the Judeo-Christian-Islamic. These resolve themselves into three models of God: you are God, and only have to realize it (Hindu); you become God (that is, an enlightened being) through your own hard effort (Buddhist); and you unite with God by participating in the divine nature (Judeo-Christian-Islamic). These goals can be expressed in two ultimate experiences: personal, intimate relationship with God, as in the theistic traditions; or a nonrelational realization of Ultimate Reality, as in Buddhism and Jainism.

Each form of meditation is about awareness, but each tradition has its own understanding of this quality of mystical awareness. Awareness requires transformation, and each school of meditation leads to this transformation. It can be observed that awareness and transformation culminate in holiness, and holiness of life is the same in all the traditions. If the fruit of the mystical journey is the same, then the Source of this delectable fruit must also be the same.

The universal interest in meditation and mysticism may well be pointing the way in our evolution. Meditation is highly uniting of persons from various traditions. People commune with the Divine and with one another. I have witnessed this phenomenon on numerous occasions, especially in centering-prayer groups. Members of these groups often come from diverse religious traditions, but when they sit together centering, they become one beyond words, beyond the words and concepts of their traditions.

There are many forms of meditation corresponding to the final goal of each of the traditions, and Marcia Z. Nelson examines each of them in this valuable book, *Come and Sit: A Week Inside Meditation Centers*. She gives us a good sense of the nature of meditation by visiting centers where the various forms it assumes in the great world religions are practiced and taught. In doing so, she makes a significant contribution to the Interspiritual Age and to the hunger for genuine spirituality.

This book will prove to be profoundly beneficial to all those seeking the deeper life of contemplation in any tradition. It meets a genuine need in our culture, and I predict that it will have a long, long life.

Wayne Teasdale
Author of *The Mystic Heart*

Acknowledgments

Many patient, wise, and generous people helped me put this book together, sharing time, resources, knowledge, and personal histories. I am grateful first of all to all the meditators who let me walk a little way with them on their wonderfully diverse paths. I am particularly grateful to those whose expertise I drew on to set me straight on the path and those who lent photos, books, and background materials. Sister Benita Jasurda of Sacred Heart Monastery offered a wealth of encouragement and resources. Sister Joyce Kemp of the Cenacle opened doors. Mary Doolen was a generous reader. Sensei Sevan Ross of the Chicago Zen Center and Margaret McKenzie of the Chicago Kwan Um Zen community straightened my Zen arrows in looking over what I wrote about Zen meditation. Zen student Barth Wright was kind enough to spend a lot of time on getting details of photo work right. Eric Lindo and Ajahn Sompoch Thitayano at Buddhadharma Buddhist Meditation Center provided pictures, instruction, and some cross-cultural consultation. Gen Kelsang Khedrub of the Vajrayana Buddhist Center taught me a little Tibetan history. Peter McLaughlin of the Shamb-hala Meditation Center of Chicago reviewed my work and opened the archive of his memory, and Meredith Dytch opened her photo archive. Paul Numrich, Ph.D., of the Park Ridge Center for the Study of Health, Faith, and Ethics, was my guide to Buddhist Chicago, looking over material dealing with the Chicago-area Buddhist centers, his field of expertise. Laleh Bakhtiar, Ph.D., of Kazi Publications was a most knowledgeable and generous guide to Sufism and Islam, offering helpful correctives to my work. Jagdish P. Dave, Ph.D., at Governors State University imparted knowledge of Sanskrit terms and shared wonderful stories and memories. Susan Timmerman gave me a ride and started me on the Sufi path. Kashfinur Heine, Ph.D., was a patient presenter, and editor, of Sufi teaching. Rachmiel Drizin welcomed me into his home and helped me with esoteric points of Judaism. Donnell Collins, a photojournalist of spirit, knows the language of light and shadow.

Still others reviewed versions of chapters that fell within their purview of expertise and interest. I was grateful to learn from Stuart Matlins, editor-in-chief and publisher of Jewish Lights Publishing; Kendra Crossen Burroughs, annotator of a new translation of the Bhagavad Gita from SkyLight Paths; Abi'l-Khayr, a font of wisdom on Sufism—student of the Sufi Order International, ordained minister in Universal Worship, and director of activities of Omega Publications; and Father Basil Pennington, abbot of the Trappist Monastery of the Holy Spirit, Conyers, Georgia. Any errors that might remain are unintended and mine alone.

At SkyLight Paths, Jon Sweeney gave me an opportunity and excuse to learn more about the world's spiritual traditions. Polly Short Mahoney valiantly and patiently stepped in to shepherd the manuscript along, addressing issues ranging from content to serial commas. Former development editor Dave O'Neal offered soothing encouragement and helpful suggestions well beyond the call of duty. Finally, I thank my children, Meg and Andy, and my husband, Bill, for practicing patience while I researched, meditated, and wrote.

To all, *namaste.*

Come and Sit

Introduction: Coming to Sit

Sitting straight with all one's heart sustains the descent into the mind that sees and accepts all that lies within.

JAMES FINLEY, *THE CONTEMPLATIVE HEART*

Where are you hurrying to?

Would you like to slow down? Can you find a little time to sit?

If you make that time, you can become aware of how much time you actually do have. As you sit, you may also discover more: more awareness, more serenity, and even more time.

Come and sit to meditate.

Meditation is exploring: sitting—but sometimes also chanting or dancing or walking—to explore the real nature of mind, body, spirit, world. Meditation is inner research.

Some say meditation is about exploring the mind and how it creates the conditions of our existence, including how we perceive time, stress, and everyday busyness in our lives. Some say it is exploring the way to God or the Absolute that forms our existence. Some say it is a glimpse of what is timeless and unchanging; others, a glimpse of change itself, of ceaseless passing and impermanence. All say that sitting to meditate is undertaking a journey that is important, even if that journey is differently understood.

3

As you begin this journey of meditation, consider yourself blessed with a great advantage: You have beginner's mind.

Beginner's Mind

"In the beginner's mind there are many possibilities; in the expert's mind there are few." So Zen Buddhist Master Shunryu Suzuki wrote in the introduction to *Zen Mind, Beginner's Mind,* a classic work on Zen meditation that helped educate the crop of Americans who now teach and practice Zen Buddhism, one branch of the 2,500-year-old, Eastern-born Buddhist religion.

The most skillful meditation practitioners retain and cultivate "beginner's mind," a mind that is clear of preconceptions, open and fresh. Over time, the practice of meditation enlarges awareness, and helps the diligent meditator to become, and remain, mindful of what contemporary Christian writer James Finley calls "the divinity of the ceaseless flow of the one, everlasting, present moment."

Suzuki's words not only offer a profound clue to the aim of meditation, but also help to dispel the preconception that meditation is an esoteric and challenging activity that only spiritually gifted and physically limber people can do after long years of solitary practice. Anyone can learn to meditate. But it takes honesty with yourself and patience. Distancing yourself from the quicksilver movement of thought requires patience, with both yourself and the process of learning to meditate.

What Is Meditation?

Virtually all the world's major religions consider meditation to be a means of spiritual growth and a way of apprehending the Divine. Meditation is a process for deepening awareness; it is not itself a religion.

Across religious traditions, meditation has common aims and some shared techniques. But it also differs in specifics according to religious tradition.

You can think of meditation as a kind of mental housecleaning, helping you to discipline thoughts in order to enhance your ability to pay attention to whatever you are doing, whether it be walking the dog or expressing devotion to the Divine. And just as there are many ways to clean house, there are many ways to meditate.

Cleaning is most effectively done when the cleaner is comfortable with and adept at the method through practice. So it is with meditation. Different ways suit different temperaments.

A lot has been written about meditation. To explore different methods and learn to meditate, you could begin with any one of the more than two thousand books available on the subject. If you chipped away at the pile, going through one book a week, you'd be ready to start in just under forty years.

Or would you prefer to have a look inside seven different meditation centers to see what's going on and get some introductory information about what might suit you best?

This book offers you the second path. Come and sit. Come and experience. Meditation is learned through experience.

What This Book Offers

This book opens the doors of numerous meditation centers and groups that teach and use seven different meditation methods. You can take a look at what people are doing and find out what it means. You can also find out why they meditate, through stories shared by practitioners who are seasoned and committed, as well as by those who are new to meditation. In addition, you will get an introduction to the spiritual traditions that have used meditation for many hundreds of years as a tool for spiritual growth and understanding.

In this book, meditation is presented as a spiritual activity, but meditation is not necessarily spiritual for everybody who practices it. People meditate to reduce the stress of their lives and their work, improve their concentration, decrease their blood pressure, or increase their productivity. Eastern spiritual sages have long known what Western scientific sages are now measuring in controlled clinical studies: Meditation has observable, beneficial effects.

These are all good reasons to meditate, but they are separate from the scope of this book, which presents meditation in the original sense, the way it has been historically practiced: a process for spiritual growth and expression. Meditation takes the seeker inward, where mind and spirit interplay and where mystics know that Truth can be known.

This book is for you if you are spiritually curious and interested in a more disciplined spiritual exploration. It is directed to people who want to know a little more, who believe they are ready for the journey of quiet intensity that meditation will take them on.

To gather material for this book, I spoke to spiritual seekers around the United States, concentrating particularly in meditation centers and circles throughout the metropolitan Chicago area, which is blessed with a large and diverse spiritual community. Chicago is home to Sufis, Buddhists, Hindus, Christians, and Jews—the five main religious traditions represented here. It contains meditation centers, temples, monasteries, retreat houses, and many living rooms where in different ways different people come together to meditate, to worship, to study, and to explore spirituality and the way to the Divine.

In some instances, the places I visited are local centers of national networks of schools of meditation. In other cases, people meditating in Chicago-area living rooms are doing the same things they would be doing in sitting groups in San Francisco or Boston. So while the settings are unique, the experiences illustrate typical and common things in each meditation tradition.

Not everyone will have ready access to established meditation settings. Some serious meditators practice on their own, traveling occasionally to major centers for retreats or conferences. Jewish meditators, for example, have very few major U.S. centers for instruction, but circles of meditators or meditation teachers can be located by using those central resources and other sources of information about Jewish spirituality.

For those who may be studying the Jewish Kabbalah in Alaska or the Buddhist Dhammapada in North Dakota, books and other media, such as instructional tapes and videos, are plentiful and accessible resources. Internet access is another valuable avenue as the presence of spiritual sites on the Web becomes more common. The Web is one way of furnishing resources and also a way of building a community. Chat groups and bulletin boards can link those with common interests but disparate locations.

In this book, specialized resource lists at the end of each chapter, and a list of "multitradition" resources in chapter 8, include selected key works and periodicals, locations of major centers and other organizations that teach or promote meditation, and Internet-based information about meditation. None of these lists is comprehensive. They are intended only to get you started with major sources.

In observing, researching, and practicing meditation, I have tried to pay attention to the similarities and differences in who meditates, why they meditate, and what they do. Some of the similarities across paths, techniques, and experiences are striking. The meditators I met had some traits and desires in common. Perhaps as you begin this journey, you can recognize yourself among those already traveling.

Who Meditates?

Not everyone is drawn to meditation. Some people don't want to sit still or don't think they can. Many people are impatient, results oriented, or make decisions based on bottom-line or cost-benefit calculations. Meditation is slow and involves opening up, rather than closing in on a goal. Many meditative paths ask you to give up a goal and experience detachment. Meditation focuses on a receding horizon, and the question "When do we get there?" is better posed on a vacation trip than on a spiritual journey.

Many of the meditators I met told me that they consciously set themselves on a new spiritual path because of dissatisfaction with the religion—or in a few instances, the lack of religion—of their childhood. They were missing some important spiritual element in their lives. Some of them were put off by what they perceived as rigidity, punitiveness, or irrelevance of the beliefs and practices they were first taught. They found rote beliefs or "holiday religion" insubstantial and incapable of answering deeper questions.

Not everyone who meditates comes to it from spiritual rebellion, however. Some have stayed within the spiritual tradition in which they were raised. Yet they sought a renewed and deeper understanding of their tradition and a revitalized, more meaningful practice. Their religion met their spiritual needs in an enriched way because of what meditation added: a sense of quiet, immediate, and unmediated connection, and greater depth. Meditation made the tradition alive.

Many meditators also told me that meditation satisfied a longstanding inclination or penchant. "I've always had a deep calling or attraction for the contemplative life," said one woman, who had spent six years in a Catholic convent. Another man dated his curiosity about Buddhism back to a high school history project about Buddhist sculpture, which fascinated him.

A number of people I met became acquainted with other religious and spiritual paths in the course of their education. Some of them studied world religions or comparative religions in college; a number of those drawn to Buddhism began their practice during that time of exposure, in very early adulthood, when people are often consciously constructing adult identities.

Even more common was the phenomenon of "shopping" among traditions for the best spiritual fit. I heard often of people's shift from one form to another: Tibetan to Zen, Sufism to Buddhism, Eastern spirituality to Christian centering prayer. Similarly, even after finding a form that satisfies their needs, many meditators remain open to learning from other approaches or combinations of approaches, in such varied forms as Zen-Christian retreats, acknowledgment of universalism within spiritual seeking, and varied interfaith activities. This kind of openness and accumulated experience and familiarity with other paths gives meditators spiritual literacy. It also makes for a high degree of tolerance of other paths. Many espoused the "perennial wisdom" philosophy: The great spiritual figures of different religious traditions all preached similar truths.

So many seekers and people interested in spirituality are both curious and open; they question, search, try. This pattern, as Kwan Um Zen Master Seung Sahn might say, is not good, not bad. It is certainly a way to develop a personally meaningful practice, but it may detract from the commitment that is necessary in any and all practices. In a recorded conversation, journalist Bill Moyers and world religions scholar Huston Smith put the question this way: Is it better to dig one ninety-foot well, or nine ten-foot ones? Each meditator unearths his or her own answer.

The Hard Way

None of the meditative paths is easy; all of them take time and effort. All of them bring dry times, dark nights of the soul, distractions, hasty judgments—the squirreled-away regrets of the soul or mistakes of the past coming to the surface of awareness as the process of meditation turns on inner lights. These are so many illusions and temptations, most teachers would say; there are even special terms in a number of traditions for these kinds of compelling mental confusions. Don't let them stop you.

So many meditators I met as I researched this book had tried a variety of approaches before finding the right fit. If at first you don't succeed at finding what feels right, try, try again. Anything is possible, but nothing is easy. Meditation is a way, but not a shortcut. Over and over I heard this from students whose practice was long-term and steady: You have to do the work. "The path we are discussing," writes Tibetan Buddhist teacher Chogyam Trungpa in *Cutting through Spiritual Materialism,* "is called the hard way."

So if you think that meditation is a way to get someplace fast, chances are you won't get to that place, or anywhere else, by meditating. If, on the other hand, meditation strikes you as a path for slowing down, then you are heading in the right direction.

The awakening that meditation brings is gradual. *Awakening* is a term commonly used to describe what meditation does; *Buddha* means "awakened one." Awakening is comprehensive and experiential. We awaken our capacities, awaken to meaning, awaken to the ubiquitous presence of the Divine, awaken to every day, awaken to the reality that is right in front of our noses, that is in our very noses with each breath we inhale and exhale.

Meditation Techniques: "Aiming for One or Zero"

Just as meditators have common characteristics, so do their paths, even while following different spiritual traditions. In *The Meditative Mind: The Varieties of Meditative Experience,* Daniel Goleman cites insight meditation teacher Joseph Goldstein: "All meditation systems either aim for One or Zero—union with God or emptiness."

Sometimes, meditation involves concentration on a single focal point. In the Hindu tradition, a mantra—a sacred sound—is used; some Jewish meditation practices focus on the letters of the Hebrew alphabet in an attempt to penetrate a deeper level of meaning. Buddhists meditate on certain utterances to develop compassion. Christian centering prayer uses a "sacred word," not as a focus but as a kind of anchor to which the meditator returns when distracted by passing thoughts.

Meditation can also open the mind up to a greater awareness of impermanence or change, to the motion of thoughts arising and passing away. The meditator practices not clinging to any mental construction; insight meditation teaches this, as does centering prayer. This kind of practice teaches the meditator a lot about the mind and its workings, and about the mind's interaction with the world.

Breath awareness is important in any meditation. Some traditions offer an education about the breath and its role in our well-being. One common meditation technique is to bring the attention to the point between the nostrils, where breath enters and exits the body, as a focal point. In the Hindu tradition, different exercises for manipulating the breath can change the flow of energy—*prana*—through the body. Sufis teach purification by breath. Beginners in Zen are taught to count their breath to help stabilize the wandering mind.

Breath is the bridge between body and mind, the way to open the mind anew and refresh the body with what it needs to do its work. It is a powerful symbol—*ruach* in Judaism, *prana* in the Hindu tradition, the breath of life celebrated in poetry and sacred story—that is immediate proof of a reality we cannot see. We cannot see our breath and are usually not conscious of it, yet our lives depend on it and we breathe without ceasing. This basic insight provided by breath is readily available and profound, a beginner's clue to the unorthodox ways of perception that meditation cultivates. It is an accessible first step toward greater awareness.

Meditation is invariably pictured as silent and seated, but this is not always so. Sufi *dhikr* (remembrance of God) may include vocal repetition of God's name. Sufi dancing is meditation, a means of fixing the mind on the beloved and the qualities of the Divine Beloved. Some Jewish meditation may involve chanting, dancing, or other body movements. Chanting is important in Buddhism and may open or close a meditation session. Hindu mantras may be said silently or uttered aloud. Certain sounds are considered sacred; they can be felt in the body and are associated with energy centers.

Given differences in techniques and in spiritual frames of reference, different people will find some kinds of meditation more congenial than others, as I did. Familiarity with a spiritual tradition can be an advantage because it answers basic questions and minimizes the distractions bred by unfamiliarity. But beginner's mind is always an advantage, as long as the meditator is comfortable, unintimidated, and receptive.

Common Questions among Beginners

Beginning meditators encounter many questions and opportunities. One frequent area of concern is the role of a teacher. What does the teacher do? Do I need one? How can I find a good one?

While it is possible to begin without a teacher, as many of the meditators I spoke with did, it's not possible to make serious progress without one. Teachers are guides with different specific functions and meanings in different traditions. Teachers provide occasions to learn deeply about meditation, about the self, about the big questions that nag at people who are drawn to meditation.

In many traditions, the teacher-student pairing can itself be a vehicle for teaching and for self-exploration. Or the teacher may function as the representation of a spiritual master. In a chapter on choosing a teacher in *A Path with Heart: A Guide through the Perils and Promises of Spiritual Life,* well-known insight meditation teacher Jack Kornfield writes, "Like choosing a partner in marriage, choosing a teacher also asks for a deep respect of our own inner knowing, and a willingness to commit when the circumstances seem right."

Clarity in this relationship is important because the student becomes vulnerable. As a path of self-exploration, meditation encourages openness and increases our willingness to encounter new possibilities. The disciplined meditator may pierce through ordinary psychological self-defenses. Spiritual traditions talk about the discomfort—at times, acute spiritual distress—that often accompanies increased awareness, leaving an individual more raw or susceptible. Profound meditation alters consciousness; that is one reason why people do it. A dependable and knowledgeable guide can give information and reassurance. Some traditions also talk about "spiritual friends" as useful support.

Someone wisely said to me in the course of preparing this book that the teacher in front of you is the one you fall in love with. In fact, I "fell in love" repeatedly with many skillful teachers in a number of different traditions. It is important for practical, emotional, and spiritual reasons to trust the teacher. Yet it's understandably easy to idealize a teacher, who at first blush appears to be an embodiment of accomplishment, however ostensibly humble. A teacher's authority should set a measure of distance between master and student without lessening the depth of the relationship.

Spiritual mastery aside, teachers are still on their own paths, albeit often farther down the road to self-realization. And so like everything else involving humans, the teacher-student relationship has occasionally been abused. Teachers have violated ethics in common human ways: sexual misconduct, alcoholism, deceit. As a result, some centers have had to deal with the consequences of such abuse of authority. Some have developed codes of conduct and ethics for teachers. Insight meditation teachers, for example, follow a set of guidelines.

The beginning student can and should be prudent without being rigidly defensive. One reassurance can be found in the tradition or lineage of a teacher. Lineage shows you a teacher's teachers, in a chain that stretches back into a spiritual tradition. In addition to defining a unique spiritual approach, lineage provides a spiritual reference for a center or teacher. Any legitimate tradition is filled with multiple voices that enrich interpretation, add fresh views, and make the teaching a living tradition that still has relevance to everyday life no matter how long ago that teaching and tradition began, no matter how different was the way of life at the tradition's birth.

Conversely, then, a center's or group's reliance on a single teacher to the exclusion of all other voices can be seen as a red flag. Centers or groups without room for more than one voice and interpretation are, at best, incomplete or exclusive; at worst, they have something other than enlightenment in mind.

A second area for prudent decision-making is financial. Enlightenment is priceless, but the journey to it always has some cost. Traditions and centers differ about the real question of how much to charge for instruction in meditation and what "paying" means. For example, insight meditation, drawn from the Theravada Buddhist tradition, tries to incorporate *dana*, a Sanskrit and Pali term that means "donation" or "alms." Historically, monks possessed almost nothing; they were to beg for their subsistence as part of their spiritual practice. In return, they provided spiritual instruction. This practice has been adopted or adapted by some spiritual teachers, notably within the insight meditation community; some centers charge fees for expenses, but teachers are paid through *dana*.

Western ways, however, invariably govern Western spiritual centers and teachers. Some make it a spiritual point to make instruction affordable. Many centers have baskets and envelopes out for donations, leaving the matter to the discretion of the student. The cost of retreats, instruction, and spiritual "accessories," such as cushions and benches, is often the subject of discussion among practitioners concerned about, in Chogyam Trungpa's apt summary term, *spiritual materialism.* Spiritual materialism can pile up the books and pillows, which lead nowhere if unused. It makes sense to start small and stay simple along the path, watching as the way opens.

Finding the Way

My own way has opened very slowly. Some years back now, when I was a young adult, I tried meditating. At that time, the late 1970s, it seemed a pretty mysterious proposition. I wanted peace of mind and respite from neuroses aggravated by work life and unworkable relationships. Meditation appeared to promise a way. I chose a Hindu path, buying books and taking classes in yoga, which taught me both the physical postures of hatha yoga and the discipline of meditation.

Physically, sitting was not difficult. I could fold fairly easily into a full-lotus position and attend to the movement of my breath. But the mental part was challenging. I thought I was not supposed to think, and I found that very difficult. I kept thinking. The thoughts simply kept coming. I couldn't find the tap inside my brain and turn it off.

I thought I must be doing something wrong. I thought I was the only one with this problem. I was somewhat intimidated by the foreign cultural context in which I was learning. My thinking continued. It seemed as if nothing was happening. I wasn't "advancing," and enlightenment began to seem impossible. And so, despite the fact that I was a decent, disciplined, flexible student of yoga, I gave it up.

Some years and life events later, through the discipline of the silent worship of Quakers, I found my way back to meditation. In 1991, when

I began attending Quaker meetings—as our worship gatherings are called—I found it difficult to sit in a group of people who might remain silent for an entire hour, as is the Quaker way. Once again, my mind would go for a walk, or many walks, starting off in one direction, then another. But over time and with repetition and the focused spiritual power of a group providing a supportive and appropriate environment, I began to learn to discriminate among the various things springing up mentally in the course of sitting quietly. More important, I learned patience: patience with habit, patience with silence, patience with my own expectations, patience with ambiguity and open-endedness.

Today, I expect less and get more. I heard, again and again, as you may: When the student is ready, the teacher will appear. The way will open.

This book is not intended to teach you *how* to meditate. I am not a meditation teacher. I am a student of meditation, and of the world's religions. I am also a journalist with a specialty in religion, trained in observing, questioning, and translating into everyday English the special languages often used within religion. So use this book as you knock on the doors of different centers, as you consider different teachers, as you try different paths.

This book follows certain conventions worth clarifying. In visiting centers, I spoke with numerous teachers and students. Some of the students were beginners; all of the teachers were also students. Although I have included the first and last names of center directors, administrators, or significant contacts, for the most part the people in this book are referred to by first names only. This is intended to minimize confusion, but it is also meant to make your exploration a little friendlier. It serves, too, to make the experience of the meditators less tied to unique individual experiences and egos. Meditation, after all, often moves us to the experience of oneness.

A note on spelling and the many foreign words encountered within world spiritual traditions: I have followed the standard practice in books for general readers of omitting diacritical marks when using English translations or transliterations of foreign terms. All foreign words are defined on first usage in the text. A glossary in the back serves as an at-a-glance compendium of foreign terms.

* * *

When I was researching and writing this book, I had this dream: I was in a large, hotel-like public building looking for a large gathering—a conference, or perhaps a high school reunion—I was to attend. I passed through banquet room after banquet room, looking for just the right place where I belonged. I always knew where I was headed, but walking and looking seemed to take a long time.

Having meditated regularly as an essential part—the experiential part—of my research, I wasn't surprised to have a dream with such clear significance. Like meditation, dreams are a time-honored tool of spiritual development. My dream told me that each religious tradition offers a rich feast; each has attractions and sustenance. Although I could pass through many rooms, however, I really belonged in only one. And, I discovered, once I got there, it was not what I had expected.

If you are searching for the banquet to which you have been invited, your challenge is to find out where it is. It may not be what you expect; you may discover many alternatives along the way. But you have been invited, and you do belong.

Welcome to the many possibilities. Taste and see.

1

Centering Prayer: Resting in God's Presence

When we experience the presence of God, if we can just not think about it, we can rest in it for a long time.

THOMAS KEATING, *OPEN MIND, OPEN HEART*

Arriving

This is the bridge that it's time to cross, now that I've come to it. The white wooden structure is right in front of me. It's dark, and the lights in the building just ahead look inviting.

Narrow as a creek, the DuPage River flows under the bridge. The river's current hustles along, visible in reflected spots of light on water. Gleaming punctuation marks, the lights define the stream's surface and penetrate the water's depth. But their waterborne reflections are an illusion, teasing likenesses of the real things, mounted lamps glowing like sentries at either end of the bridge.

Here at the Cenacle Retreat House and Spirituality Center, located in the suburb of Warrenville, just thirty miles west of busy downtown Chicago, they call this the Bridge of Hope. Many who come to this forty-two-acre place of peace and quiet are immediately struck, as I was, by the symbolism of the bridge. I came in the dark and crossed over to the

Retreatants cross the Bridge of Hope to a time of renewal and reflection at the Cenacle Retreat House and Spirituality Center in Warrenville, Illinois. The Cenacle, like other retreat centers, offers a refuge from the frenzied world. It is welcoming and accessible, yet removed from the busyness of everyday life. (Photo: Donnell Collins)

light, my quick, silent steps swallowed by darkness, cushioned by the wooden planks of the bridge.

This place could be God's hotel. Several large common rooms are comfortably appointed, offering spots for conversation or solitary reading or reflection. Up carpeted stairs, a long hallway is punctuated by many doors leading to small single rooms, provided for people on retreats.

At the end of the hallway is the Upper Room, named after the place where the disciples of Jesus prayed after his ascension. The second-floor Upper Room is a large windowed space, lit by a sanctuary candle and a subdued spotlight shining on a golden oak tabernacle, a small cabinet used by Catholics to house the consecrated hosts given out for Holy Communion. Both Jews and Catholics understand a tabernacle as the dwelling place of God.

One side of the tabernacle is inset with a rose-colored, sunlike mandala, a sacred symbol, rendered in stained glass. The purpose of the circular mandala is to invite the beholder on a journey—visual, mental, and spiritual—that winds its way inside, to a center. The center symbolizes the sacred source from which all creation flows. Behind the tabernacle on the wall are three painted chevrons, tentlike and welcoming. The last of winter's blooming poinsettias, arranged here, are dappled pink, pale as the season. A hefty Bible is cracked open on a bookstand. A lectern is draped with a clerical stole. All the items speak symbolically, inviting reflection.

This is the room where a centering-prayer group gathers weekly to pray together silently, to journey within to sit in the Lord's presence. Five or six people are already seated in the quiet, dimly lit room, most of them sitting upright in chairs, feet flat on the floor. A few choose to sit cross-legged on the floor amid cushions, in traditional Eastern style. People hold their hands in different positions. Some rest their hands on their thighs, turning their palms upright, slightly cupped. Others rest their hands in their laps, placing left hand over right, palms up, thumbs lightly joined and pointed upward. The session begins, without signal or sound. The group prays for twenty minutes, and then does a five-minute contemplative walk, slowly and in silence. A second twenty-minute centering-prayer period concludes the session.

It is totally quiet for the forty-five-minute meditation, except for the unobtrusive sound of a small bell that marks the end of each sitting period. People in the group know one another, but the room is not a place for socializing. Talk is reserved for outside; this place, the Upper Room, is reserved for silence, which many mystics have said is the speech of God.

To Be Instead of To Do

For those steeped in everyday noisiness and chatty sociability, all this silence may take a little getting used to. But many of those who practice centering prayer say that they were prompted to begin by a craving for silence, a yearning that the practice satiates and then deepens. When I first came to the Upper Room, I felt a great sense of relief, as if I could relax and shed my everyday, functional shell. Settling into silence offers comfort: a chance to grow comfortable with being nowhere, with having nobody to impress and nothing to do. Just be—sit in God's presence, just as I would with a dear and accepting friend. Take off the mask—centering-prayer practitioners call it "the false self"—and sit in the silence, without trying to accomplish anything, not even the perfection of the practice itself. Some would call this heretical suggestion "wasting time for God." Mary, a member of the group that gathers at the Cenacle, says that centering prayer is like climbing into her own bed, into a familiar sense of deep relationship.

"Here I am," she says. "It's like coming home to ourselves."

We know a lot more about doing than being. Doing is, well, going about our duties or whatever we have convinced ourselves needs to get done each day or otherwise regularly. From the viewpoint of productive society, being is pretty useless, even lazy. It does not contribute to the enlargement of the gross national product and an individual paycheck's worth of it. Giving ourselves permission to just be can be difficult. Many practitioners of centering prayer report initial resistance to the discipline until it begins to seem first natural and later necessary for well-being.

Centering prayer brings a brief period of withdrawal from the world's busyness, a practice that dates back to a time when the world was a lot less busy than it is now. Rooted in the Christian monastic and contemplative tradition and developed to fit within today's active lifestyles, centering prayer fosters the experience of God through interior

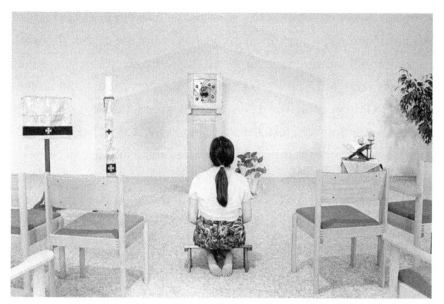

Centering prayer is practiced in silence, which some say is the speech of God. Most practitioners sit in chairs, but some sit on cushions or use meditation benches, as shown in this photo. (Photo: Donnell Collins)

journey. Centering prayer not only takes us away from the world but also stills personal, habitual, continual mental chatter, in order to behold the sound of God within inner silence.

Many scripture passages associate God with silence:

> Be still before the Lord and wait patiently for him. (Psalm 37:7)
> Be still, and know that I am God. (Psalm 46:10)
> After the earthquake came a fire, but the Lord was not in the fire. And after the fire came a gentle whisper. (1 Kings 19:12)

Silencing Ourselves

Like any form of meditation, centering prayer is a method for silencing ourselves by stopping the usual stream of thought. Consistent with

Christian belief, it takes God as its focus, seeking to raise awareness of divine indwelling presence in all things. It does not use images, thoughts, or traditional formal prayer or words, with the exception of a single, short "sacred word," which is chosen by the practitioner and uttered silently to initiate centering prayer, and which may be used periodically during prayer time to return the mind to God, should it begin wandering. It is not concentration, which implies effort and use of the will; rather, it is a way of directing and increasing inner attention. Centering prayer makes a person a disciple relaxed in the presence of the master, or a child resting securely in the presence of a parent. "Resting in God" is a common description used by centering-prayer teachers.

> You don't have to *do* anything. Just rest in God's arms. It is an exercise in *being* rather than *doing*. (Thomas Keating, *Open Mind, Open Heart*)

Many people lose a sense of time and place during centering prayer. When I close my eyes and progressively loosen my grip on habitual thought flow, I have an intimation of being alive but being nowhere, being nothing but my breath, breath of life replacing stream of thought.

Maura, who began centering prayer eleven years ago when she was pregnant with her youngest child, experiences it, she says, "as a resting in God, letting go of concerns and words and sitting still with God—no more, no less." She adds, "Sometimes that's difficult, sometimes that's easy."

What Practitioners Say

Mary: "keeping in touch with God and myself"

Practiced habitually, centering prayer certainly yields practical byproducts, like cutting down on fidgeting and fuming in lines and traffic jams. It lengthens patience, abridges boredom. It brings the white light of clarity, unbidden, to the mind at other times throughout the day.

"We have these moments of clarity as a result of those moments of quiet," says Mary, a ten-year practitioner of centering prayer. "I know that's ideal, but I do believe it's true."

But that's not why she does it. Mary practices it because it keeps her in touch with God and with herself. To know herself is to know more about who God the Creator made her to be. It gives her "a felt sense of faith," an experience of the presence of God.

Mary, a fifty-nine-year-old business owner, part-time spiritual director, and mother of four grown children, has blonde hair, and her blue eyes wrinkle up when she smiles. Her face has experience lines. She wears a thick black sweater against the chill that can steal up in the stillness of silent prayer. She coughs—right now she's battling a seasonal cold—but centering prayer is important to do regularly. Doing it with a group helps her discipline.

"It's a gift to want to do it," she says. Her wanting began with a little reading, with going to conferences where she heard Christian teachers and writers like Henri Nouwen, Richard Foster, and James Finley—explorers of silence, of prayer, of disciplined development of faith. That helped nurture her desire. But doing was better than reading. She didn't read the books of Thomas Keating, one of the founders of centering prayer, until she was on her way to a workshop at the Colorado monastery where he lives. "I don't think I read it through till I was on the train that night," she confesses. To retain her motivation and refresh her practice, once a year she treats herself to a quiet retreat.

She looks at her own life for evidence of the results—the fruit—of centering prayer. "In retrospect," she says, "I could see a lot of things change in my life. Do I know it at the time? No. It's part of a process that enables me to grow."

Kathy: "hungering for God's presence"

Kathy, who is fifty-six, has been coming for three years to centering-prayer meetings at the Cenacle. "I've always had a deep calling or attraction to the contemplative life," she says. When she was younger, she spent six years in a Carmelite order, but left. She also studied dance and art; today, she continues to paint. One of her works, an eleven-foot-tall picture of the risen Christ, hangs in her home church, a Catholic parish.

"There's a tension," says Kathy, who is now a home-care nurse, "between being busy and taking the time to do nothing useful but sit in God's presence. I hunger for that now."

Like Mary, Kathy has begun to enjoy the fruits of her practice at times in her day that have little to do with being quiet. It shows up when she's driving to work with greater calmness. It's changed the way she washes the dishes, makes the bed. "It's all connected to centering prayer."

Bob: "developing a discipline"

Bob is a beginner at centering prayer, learning it through a five-week class that he happens to be in charge of because the class is offered through the parish he works for. He comes to it out of interest in exploring this form of prayer, which is so different than the more typical active forms of prayer. His first taste of centering prayer is good enough to make him want to pursue more following the five-week class in order to develop a discipline. "As you explore different possibilities or modes of prayer, some will appeal to you, some won't appeal," he says. "I'm surprised this does." He guesses with a laugh that its quietness is more appealing to him because he is aging—he is forty-six. Keating has suggested that centering prayer "takes" better among older people, who have accumulated, or suffered through, more experience.

Elizabeth: "Struggling is part of growth"

Elizabeth does centering prayer in spite of herself. "I'm fifty-seven," she explains. "It's taken fifty-seven years for my mind to get where it is, and it doesn't want to let anyone in to change it, not even God."

Elizabeth "blames" Ted, the rector of her Episcopal parish in downtown Chicago. "Ted made me do it," she says with good humor. "He said, 'This would be good for you.'"

And it is, she concedes, but it's a difficult discipline. She is aware of her resistance to the practice and has taken steps around that resistance. "I find any excuse not to do it, so I've arranged to lead it three times a week," she says. She and a friend have a centering-prayer "buddy system," exchanging calls daily as a gentle reminder to sit for centering prayer.

Centering-prayer practitioners encounter and acknowledge resistance and try to work with it. Struggling against that resistance is part of the growth within the practice, Elizabeth believes. "Every time we fight the resistance, some change happens," she suggests.

Elizabeth, who describes herself as a spiritual director and grandmother, began centering prayer two years ago, and early in 2001 attended a ten-day intensive centering-prayer retreat at St. Benedict's Monastery in Snowmass, Colorado, where Keating now lives and works.

"It was just otherworldly," she says. She participated in five hours of centering prayer daily. "It's quiet. It puts your whole soul in a different place.... You leave saying, 'That's how I want my world to be,' but that's not how it is."

Renewing Christian Tradition

Centering prayer was developed in the 1970s by Trappist monks Thomas Keating, William Meninger, and M. Basil Pennington, all then at St. Joseph Abbey in Spencer, Massachusetts. Blending aspects of Eastern meditation with traditional Christian belief and prayer form, centering prayer represents an attempt to draw new attention to Christianity's own mystical tradition in order to feed contemporary spiritual hunger for a direct experience of the Divine.

While the current form of centering prayer is contemporary, it is rooted in centuries of Christian contemplative practice. The practice represents a response to the perennial spiritual question: How shall I pray? For Christians, the answer begins with Jesus, who offers this instruction:

> When you pray, go into your room, close the door, and
> pray to your Father, who is unseen. (Matthew 6:6)

Jesus' answer to the question is the basis of the teaching and prayer of church fathers and other thinkers who followed the path of prayer as a means of connection with God. In tracing the history of this practice, Keating, Meninger, and Pennington reach all the way back to the desert fathers, monks of the fourth and fifth centuries who lived, taught, and prayed in the deserts of Palestine and Egypt.

In the monastic scheme of things, contemplation was the climactic step of a divine ladder of processes that built a relationship to God. Four separate but related practices made up *lectio divina,* meant to provide an encounter with the Divine through sacred text. *Lectio divina*—reading of the sacred scripture—brought the reader a small portion of divinely inspired word, meant to be read slowly, ruminatively. Reading led naturally to *meditatio,* thoughtful reflection stimulated by the scripture passage just read. *Meditatio* could involve simple repetition of the passage in order to assimilate its meaning. The gradual interior movement toward God then led to *oratio,* understood as prayer, a felt response to the growing understanding of God that naturally produced praise. The final step of the process was then *contemplatio,* contemplation, or coming to rest in the presence of God.

One important work within the Christian mystical tradition is prominent in the history of centering prayer. The fourteenth-century text *The Cloud of Unknowing*, written by an unknown author, takes the form of advice given by an experienced monk to a younger pupil who is eager to develop his spiritual life. The older teacher gives his student specific instructions for prayer. The writer advises his disciple to sit quietly, center his attention on God, and use a short, simple word that will help attention stay centered on God. The word is intended to represent God, and it is also used to return the mind to the presence of God when, almost inevitably, the distraction of thoughts starts.

The value of contemplative practices changed over time, with the development of new teachings about prayer and with the eclipse of monasticism by more active and worldly lifestyles. But even while this form of prayer remained the heart of the Christian contemplative tradition, the institutional church and its authorities began to look askance at the practice of contemplation, eventually walling it off in monasteries for the select few, although earlier it had been understood as a natural spiritual development open to anyone faithful.

Other postmedieval church writers, among them the Spaniard John of the Cross, a sixteenth-century teacher of prayer, influenced the development of contemplative prayer. John, a contemporary of Teresa of Avila, known for her ecstatic prayer life, was imprisoned twice by the Inquisition because of his interest in mystical theology. His highly literary work is significant in Western mysticism.

The founders of centering prayer draw on this part of Christian heritage, and they also acknowledge a more contemporary debt to Thomas Merton, a Trappist monk and a profound and prolific author. Merton was familiar with the Western monastic tradition as well as streams of mysticism within non-Western traditions, including Zen, Taoist, and Sufi spiritual wisdom. Over time, Merton increasingly incorporated his understanding of the spiritual heart of Eastern religious traditions into his writings for Western readers. His work gave rise to the term *centering prayer*.

> Monastic prayer begins not so much with "considerations" as with a return to the heart, finding one's deepest center, awakening the profound depths of our being in the presence of God, who is the source of our being and our life. (Thomas Merton, *The Climate of Monastic Prayer,* Cistercian Publications, 1969)

Beyond Catholicism

Ted: *"nurturing a silent relationship to God"*

While the founders of centering prayer are Catholic, other Christians also feel at home with it. "There's nothing I find that would be heretical or upsetting" to Episcopalians, says Ted, Elizabeth's Episcopal priest, who is a six-year practitioner of centering prayer.

Paradoxically enough, he came to the practice by way of an Eastern tradition. Eight years ago, he began studying tai chi, a practice of movement and silence that "opened up my body, and opened me to quiet," he says. "I went East to go West."

He then encountered centering prayer "by accident," he says. He was visiting a friend who was familiar with it, and that friend drew him into the practice.

"It was just exactly what I needed," he says. "It was a godsend, so to speak."

Ted, who is forty-seven, finds centering prayer especially fruitful at his time of life, as his energy level shifts and his concerns mellow and change with age. His hairline is receding, and pounds as well as experience are beginning to accumulate on him. His awareness, and concerns, are changing.

"In my mid-forties, I'm starting to ask, 'Who am I, what am I doing, whom am I doing it with?'"

Less philosophically, centering prayer is also a change of pace for this cleric. As a priest, Ted does a lot of talking about God and the Spirit. Centering prayer offers an opportunity for a radically different, silent relationship to God. "It's so stimulating and refreshing to just shut up," he says with a laugh.

Ted, who leads groups and teaches them as an area coordinator for the Chicago centering-prayer network, also finds his practice a spiritually refreshing change from traditional Episcopal worship, another major activity in his life. Sometimes, the liturgy can feel like a horse race. "Bam! You're off, quick, jump up," he says. "Can't we just sit sometimes?"

Pat: "redeveloping my relationship to God"

One of Ted's parishioners is new to centering prayer. Pat began six months ago, prompted to it by Ted and other practitioners in her church. The good news for her is that it's calming; the bad news is that it's difficult.

"It's hard to sit and be still," this animated woman confesses. "I'm thinking of all this stuff. It's been a challenge, but the more I do it, the easier it gets."

Pat, who is thirty-eight, came to her new church home a year ago as part of her spiritual journey. She had been visiting Catholic churches, the faith in which she was raised; her brother is a priest. "I needed to redevelop my relationship with God," she explains. "I knew I needed church in my life." Meditation was a new spiritual element for her, although she had practiced some yoga and concentration meditation.

Her centering-prayer practice has already produced tangible results. "When I do it," she says, "my day is completely different." And she has already worked through some issues that plague beginners at centering prayer or any other meditative practice: the "how-am-I-doing syndrome," a tendency to check progress or worry about doing it correctly.

"I did that at the very beginning," she says. "I got over whether I'm 'doing it right.'"

Elizabeth, also a member of this Episcopal parish, says that the references in centering prayer circles can sometimes seem fairly Catholic, but not exclusively so. "I have a sense of humor about it," she says. Her experience in an intensive centering-prayer workshop was "very neutral" with respect to denomination, she says.

Hal: "God is all that counts"

Hal is an ordained Methodist minister who calls himself "a spiritual Catholic." "In terms of being Catholic or Protestant, it doesn't matter anymore," he says. "I think there's something transcending the denominations today that's bringing us to a place where God is all that counts." Hal began centering prayer five or six years ago after years of using other short traditional contemplative prayers. He began by reading Keating's *Open Mind, Open Heart,* and moved from the book to the teacher, attending a workshop at St. Benedict's, Keating's home monastery. Hal now practices centering prayer twice a day for half-hour sessions. "It forms my sanity," he says.

Hal's practice has deep roots. "I have always had a hunger for the inner journey," he says. He had what he describes as "a powerful religious experience" when he was sixteen years old that led him into ministry. He worked at churches in North Carolina, Minnesota, Southern California, and Kentucky before coming to Chicago in 1969, where he became active in ecumenical work and "marketplace ministry," developing small faith communities in the city. He is now sixty-six, and he and his wife, Betsy, teach centering prayer. The two work frequently with couples to offer instruction, spiritual direction, and dream work to uncover the spiritual significance of dreams. They are writing a book on the religious interpretation of dreams.

"I'm spending less extroverted energy and letting life come to me rather than trying to make things happen," says Hal. "When we come to that quiet center more and more, I think our unconscious draws what needs to happen."

Making mysticism modern

More Protestants than Catholics attend the centering-prayer workshops that Sister Benita offers. "Catholics might be afraid of the word 'contemplation,'" says Sister Benita, a Benedictine nun who is a trained centering-prayer teacher and another coordinator in the Chicago-area centering-prayer network. Despite the existence of a stream of tradition teaching and extolling the value of contemplation, the development of prayer practices for the Catholic faithful in the pews led toward private pietism and away from contemplation. Sitting in contemplative silence may be viewed with suspicion by some in light of an institutional history that shies away from mysticism.

So centering prayer has emerged from a reassessment of a mystical lineage within the pre-Reformation Christian tradition. It adapts ancient teachings to answer the contemporary need for a spirituality that is deep enough to provide inner peace and flexible enough to fit today's non-monastic lifestyles.

The Process

If all prayer is a conversation or relationship with God, then centering prayer is a particular kind of relationship. The practice of contemplation, says Thomas Keating,

> is primarily relationship, hence, intentionality. It is not a technique, it is prayer.... Centering prayer is a method of moving our developing relationship with God to the level of pure faith. Pure faith is faith that is moving

beyond the mental egoic level of discursive meditation and particular acts to the intuitive level of contemplation. (Thomas Keating, *Open Mind, Open Heart*)

Centering prayer has four steps that constitute a "rule," or set of guidelines to follow.

1. Begin by choosing a sacred word, a short, one- or two-syllable word that expresses an intention to draw nearer to God. The word is a sign of intention; it says that you are ready, undistracted by other things, to bring attention to God's presence. It signifies consent to God. Some examples suggested by teachers: Lord, Father, Mother, love, peace, shalom, amen.

2. Sit comfortably, whether you use a chair or one of the traditional cross-legged meditation postures. Close your eyes and say the sacred word silently as you settle into silence.

3. Whenever thoughts start up in your mind, use the sacred word to draw your attention gently back to the Divine Center. The sacred word is not a mantra, or utterance, to be repeated over and over; rather, it functions as a repetition of intention to be with God. It is important because the mind habitually tends to wander, as beginners immediately notice with dismay.

4. At the end of the prayer time, remain seated in silence for a few minutes to allow thoughts and ordinary sensations and sounds to come slowly back into focus. Some teachers recommend saying a formal prayer as a way of making the transition out of contemplative quiet.

The recommended time for a centering-prayer session is twenty minutes, twice daily, once in the morning and once in the late afternoon or early evening. Longer periods can be more difficult, especially for beginners. Repetition develops the discipline and makes it easier to attain inner silence. Centering prayer is also intended to be part of a lifestyle of people engaged in the world. The discipline of quiet is meant to complement worldly activities.

Sister Benita finds centering prayer a needed refuge from her busy days. As a Benedictine, she is a member of an order that values prayer and service as a way of life and as a way of glorifying the Creator God. She has served in the fields of teaching, religious education, and campus ministry, and now is active in her community, which runs a senior retirement complex. As subprioress and coordinator of the monastery, she assists the head of her community of forty-eight sisters and oversees its daily operations. For her, centering prayer is quite literally a godsend, slowing her down to restore balance in her life.

"To be contemplative is just to enjoy the moment," she says. "It is only from the interior life that I believe we can be effective in our everyday living."

Structures of Groups

Different centering-prayer groups may structure themselves somewhat differently, adding other related practices to the core of centering prayer. Sometimes centering prayer is combined with *lectio divina,* the process of sacred reading and reflection; Keating suggests this as a format for a centering-prayer support group. Sister Benita leads a centering prayer group that meets weekly at her Benedictine monastery. The group, averaging eight at any one session, opens its weekly session with twenty minutes of centering prayer, followed by *lectio divina* using a short passage from scripture.

The passage is read three times, and members of the group who are moved to do so may repeat a brief phrase from the passage or comment briefly. *Lectio divina* comes from a time when most believers didn't know how to read, but were read to. Repetition of phrases and the use of very short passages was a way to enhance learning the scripture, to spiritually digest it. Traditionally, *lectio divina* begins with a short reading, followed by reflection and short, spontaneous prayer. The process is meant to culminate in "resting in God," or contemplation.

Sister Benita's centering-prayer group then moves to discussion and further education about centering prayer, sometimes viewing videotapes featuring Keating, who has developed many such resources for instruction and development of the practice. The videotapes serve as a shortcut to the workshop experience, and because they are intended to be instructional, they are highly useful for introducing the practice.

Other centering-prayer groups may be completely silent. The weekly group at the Cenacle, for example, observes two twenty-minute sessions of centering, punctuated by a short and silent contemplative walk. The contemplative walk offers a physical break from sitting; it is also a chance to pay attention to the action of walking without a destination—to feel

Walking meditation—"contemplative walk"— is sometimes used in centering prayer. Labyrinths, as shown here, are literal paths for spiritual contemplation. (Photo: Donnell Collins)

deliberate, slow footfalls—with an attentiveness that is absent from the invariably hasty pace of daily life.

The Cenacle is a congenial home for centering prayer and a variety of spiritual practices. It offers a rich schedule of retreats and workshops, as well as regular brief morning and evening programs on spiritual topics. Frequently, topics cross religious sectarian lines. Christian, Zen, and Jewish meditation retreats have been offered. Staff members, who lead many of the retreats and programs, also offer spiritual direction. Built shortly before 1920, the Cenacle is run by the Religious of the Cenacle, an international community of Roman Catholic women founded in France in the early nineteenth century and dedicated to the deepening of faith. The offering of retreats and other forums for faith exploration is a logical expression of the order's mission. Between four thousand and five thousand people cross the Cenacle's Bridge of Hope each year to take part in faith refreshment.

Ten sisters are in residence at the Cenacle, which draws its name from the post-Ascension story of the followers of Jesus, who gathered together in the Upper Room, or Cenacle, to pray. There they were visited by the Holy Spirit, an event commemorated at Christian Pentecost, and empowered to offer witness to their faith in Jesus.

Centering-prayer groups such as the one at the Cenacle and at other retreat and worship houses form a growing network across the United States and in seventeen other countries. Contemplative Outreach, which maintains an international office in Butler, New Jersey, is a hub of information on local groups and on workshops and retreats offered by trained leaders. Since 1988, it has grown from an initial mailing list of eight hundred interested people to forty thousand. Prayer groups have grown from 73 to almost 250, and chapters now number 184.

"Divine Therapy"

Centering prayer is done for spiritual development, but it has psychological benefits for many practitioners. It's virtually a sure-fire technique for developing patience in the face of everyday stresses, as Kathy, a three-year practitioner, has found. It's improved her commute to work, for one thing. "A train comes by, and I don't get so darn frustrated," she says. "It's changed the way I perceive time."

But the mental and emotional changes that centering prayer can bring about can go far deeper, to the core issues of being that we are usually unaware of. Keating characterizes centering prayer as "divine therapy." Once superficial distractions and habitual thoughts are swept away, deeper issues and emotions are likely to emerge from under the wraps of repression and forgetting. This process is a natural part of spiritual growth and purification, but it can be an unsettling time. The Christian mystic John of the Cross memorably describes this common experience as "the dark night of the soul." Keating calls it "the unloading of the unconscious," and says that the rediscovery of old pain is part of the healing of pain.

> Contemplative prayer fosters the healing of these wounds. In psychoanalysis the patient relives traumatic experiences of the past and in doing so, integrates them into a healthy pattern of life. If you are faithful to the daily practice of contemplative prayer, these psychic wounds will be healed without your being retraumatized. (Thomas Keating, *Open Mind, Open Heart*)

Kathy is experiencing some of the discomfort of heightened self-knowledge that comes from the centering-prayer interior journey. Although she has experienced peace and the growth of patience over three years' time, her most recent prayer sessions have brought to the surface "the dark side of myself, which somehow is a revelation to me," she says. "I've been meditating on 'love your enemy.' I see it as that within me which needs to be embraced."

Hal has also experienced darkness within, and that experience has purged certain expectations he might have held about himself, the way life ought to work, what makes up the world. "I think that experience sets me up not to be so concerned about emptiness," he says. "Wholeness is about living in the tension between all the opposites coming to us. I think centering prayer moves us to a place of detachment *in* it instead of *away* from it. The very method of centering prayer gives us a daily practice in experience of a loving nonattachment."

"Centering prayer's not for everybody," he continues. "Centering prayer really is for people who have a commitment to walk their inner journey and go through the darkness."

The mystical tradition understands the process of inner exploration as an inevitable and beneficial purification that requires removal of ego defenses. Those defenses constitute a "false self," built up from childhood, which masks a "true self," one made in God's image—a self beyond words, thoughts, ego. The true self cannot be selfish or self-indulgent, because it is the real self God made and loves unconditionally; it is a reflection of God. Through the experience of union with God, the false self is removed.

> At that moment the point of our contact with Him opens out and we pass through the center of our own nothingness and enter into infinite reality, where we awaken as our true self. (Thomas Merton, *New Seeds of Contemplation*)

Ted, the Episcopal priest, has also been experiencing some disconcerting periods of self-awareness. Although interior concerns don't surface specifically as memories or personal issues, "I just know things are getting worked on," he says. "It's a much more seamless process."

For Maura, internal change has galvanized her ability to work actively for justice. She has chosen to concentrate her energy on the issue of the ordination of women; despite a shortage of priests, the Catholic church does not allow women to be ordained as priests.

"Centering prayer helps you to live in your truth, and that's what I really seek: truth and wisdom," she explains. "We have to have change within ourselves, and that leads us to work for justice."

Like real fruit, the fruit of centering prayer takes time to grow and ripen. Greater calmness, a longer fuse, extra patience—these kinds of qualities may not be apparent at first. What is more apparent—a really common experience for beginners—is a dawning awareness of how hard doing nothing can be. Like flies in summertime, thoughts keep coming, buzzing past, and distracting. Like water flowing, thinking won't halt on command. Doing nothing only sounds simple. Yet like any difficult art, contemplative prayer gets easier with practice. Keating advises,

> Say "yes" to everything that happens....All thoughts that come down the stream of consciousness are subject to time because they are moving objects, and every object has to go by. If you just wait and do not do anything about them, they will all pass by. (Thomas Keating, *Open Mind, Open Heart*)

The changes that practitioners experience depend partly on the intuitions that may emerge when they let communion with God leaven their lives on a regular basis. Bill has been attending centering-prayer groups at the Warrenville Cenacle for a year. A Catholic who teaches art at a nearby university, he came to centering prayer as a way of adding to the transcendental meditation he has practiced for twenty-five years. He meditates for thirty minutes in the morning and again for the same length of time in the afternoon, and has no difficulty finding this time in his daily schedule.

"It's probably one of the most legitimate activities I do during the entire day," he says. "It's something I look forward to doing, as intimate as drinking my morning coffee."

His training in transcendental meditation also gives him an additional perspective on the felt experience of centering prayer. He is comfortable in describing it as "transcendental consciousness: that place where there is no duality in thought."

The goal of his practice? He stops to consider. "I think," he says slowly, "I would like more than anything to know the love of God."

Back in the Upper Room, the bell tinkles, breaking the silence. People stand up, put on shoes and coats, and head for the door. They head back to the world of noise and light, of demands and duties. Centering prayer is not done for the end of making life easier, but life can become easier when deep prayer becomes a regular part of it, when deep prayer transforms perspective and sorts the eternal from the evanescent, and when it leads the soul to the well of living water, there to slake thirst and rest wordlessly in God.

Steps for Beginners

- Not everyone begins with books, but Thomas Keating has a number of works that offer an easy and systematic introduction to the process and speak also to the Christian tradition and theology of centering prayer. This can offer initial psychological and spiritual support at the outset of practice, when beginners have many questions.

- Two daily sessions of centering prayer, one early in the day and one late but not immediately before bedtime, help develop the commitment and the ability to find silence satisfying.

- Don't be discouraged. No disciplined path is easy. Keating tells the story of a nun who told him she had been spending time daily in contemplative prayer for fifty years. She asked him if he thought she was doing it right. He told her, "I don't know exactly what you've been doing, but whatever you're doing, keep doing it."

Selected Resources

Books

Arico, Carl. *A Taste of Silence: Centering Prayer and the Contemplative Journey.* New York: Continuum, 1999.

Finley, James. *The Contemplative Heart.* Notre Dame, Ind.: Sorin Books, 2000.

Johnston, William, ed. *The Cloud of Unknowing and the Book of Privy Counseling.* New York: Image Books, 1996.

Keating, Thomas. *Intimacy with God.* New York: Crossroad, 1994.

———. *Open Mind, Open Heart.* Rockport, Mass.: Element, 1991.

Meninger, William. *The Loving Search for God: Contemplative Prayer and the Cloud of Unknowing.* New York: Continuum, 1995.

Merton, Thomas. *New Seeds of Contemplation.* New York: New Directions, 1972.

Pennington, M. Basil. *Centering Prayer: Renewing an Ancient Christian Prayer Form.* Garden City, N.Y.: Doubleday, 1980.

Centers and organizations

Alta Retreat Center
P.O. Box 407
Driggs, ID 83422
307-353-8100
altacp@tetonvalley.net

Cenacle Retreat House and Spirituality Center
P.O. Box 797
Warrenville, IL 60555-0797
630-393-1231
www.cenacle.org

Contemplative Outreach Ltd.
P.O. Box 737
10 Park Place, Suite 2B
Butler, NJ 07405
973-838-3384
www.contemplativeoutreach.org

St. Andrew's Retreat House
257 St. Andrew's Road
Walden, NY 12586
845-778-2102
cathymc@frontiernet.net

Internet sites

- www.lectiodivina.org—Lectio Divina, a website with information about this traditional spiritual discipline.

- www.wccm.org—World Community for Christian Meditation, a website with lots of information and good links.

2

Zen Buddhist Meditation: True Emptiness

True emptiness is before thinking. Before thinking, everything does not appear and does not disappear. So the truth is just like this. Red comes, there is red; white comes, there is white.

ZEN MASTER SEUNG SAHN, *DROPPING ASHES ON THE BUDDHA*

Readying the Mind

Peace and pizza are neighbors in a little suburban shopping strip.

When I enter the Enrichment Center in Wheaton, a suburb west of Chicago, Margaret, the teacher, is getting ready to quickly transform a small storefront arts center, which is right next to a pizza joint, into a *zendo*, a hall or room in which Zen Buddhist students meditate. Away go the tables and chairs, piled up in one corner; we'll be sitting, but not in chairs. Out come mats and cushions; a wooden altar is positioned atop a table, along with candles, incense, and a small statue of the Buddha. Other people enter, introducing themselves, talking. Many have brought their own cushions or small wooden meditation benches called *seiza*s, designed for sitting in a kneeling position.

All these people, who look like regular Midwestern, middle-class citizens, are students of Zen Master Seung Sahn, founder of the Kwan Um School of Zen, a Korean school of Zen Buddhism. Virtually all the people don plain gray robes over their street clothes; gray is a color reserved for lay practitioners. Then Margaret and others put over the robe a brown *kasa* (*rakusu* in Japanese), a biblike garment signifying that the wearer has taken the five Zen precepts, rules for conduct accepted in a ceremony that marks a practitioner's formal acceptance of Buddhism. Debby, a robed student, passes out chant books. When we are ready to sit, Debby opens the altar by lighting candles and incense and taking three steps backward and bowing. The formal movements, candles, and wafting incense all help to establish an atmosphere of ritual.

Margaret tells me, the newcomer, to bow—bring my hands together prayerfully and bow my head—and step behind my mat if any part of my body falls asleep while we are sitting for two periods of *zazen*, the silent sitting meditation that is the heart of Zen Buddhist practice. She also tells me that my thoughts and breathing can eventually settle into great regularity if I repeat silently "clear mind" as I breathe in and "don't know" as I breathe out.

Margaret strikes a brass bell that has been suspended between two chairs and chants the Evening Bell Chant. She then leads us all in *Kwan Seum Bosal*, a chant about the bodhisattva, or enlightened being, of compassion, keeping rhythm by striking a gourdlike wooden instrument as we chant. The repetitive chanting helps to usher in a certain readiness of mind to sit in silence. When the sitting—two thirty-minute sessions, broken by five minutes of walking meditation—ends, we will chant, in English, the *Heart Sutra*, a key text in Buddhism that proclaims the Buddha's enlightened realization of oneness. We will also chant in Korean, broken down into accessible and intonable syllables, the *Great Dharani*, an ancient rhythmic chant that is important for its sacred sound rather than its meaning.

As I try to breathe evenly and let breath awareness replace constant and skittering thought, I smile as I realize where I am. I am sitting peace-

These Zen students wear brown rakusus, *biblike garments signifying that they have taken the five Zen precepts, rules for conduct accepted in a ceremony that marks the practitioners' formal avowal of Buddhism. One plays the* mokugyo *(fish drum), left, and the other plays the* keisu *(bowl gong), right. The* mokugyo *is used to keep cadence during chanting and the* keisu *marks the beginning and end. (Photo: courtesy of Chicago Zen Center)*

fully in a storefront Zen center that is located right next to a pizza joint in a shopping strip in the suburban American heartland; I am breathing in a perfume of pizza and incense, sitting before a statue of an Asian spiritual sage who died 2,500 years ago.

Form and Freedom

Elsewhere, in a different Zen center, some things change, some things remain the same. The Chicago Zen Center is tucked in the shadow of learned Northwestern University. The university is a crazy quilt of large institutional and small residential buildings in the cosmopolitan and diverse northern Chicago suburb of Evanston. The Zen Center fits right into this landscape. It is a big green wood-sided building from the 1920s, with an old-fashioned front porch and an inconspicuous carved wooden sign that announces "Zen Center." The house and sign are easy to miss; only the porch railing suggests the simple, calligraphic-like, distinctive Zen aesthetic.

Inside, the first order of business is to take off street shoes. No wastebasket to discard prejudices, judgments, and assumptions, but there is a rack for shoes. Sevan Ross, the center *sensei*, or principal teacher, greets eighteen of us for what he calls "a precursor to a precursor to a precursor" for Zen meditation. "But," he adds, "we have to start someplace."

The interior is more like what I would expect of a Zen location: on the floor, a thick lacquer-red and cream Oriental rug with a Japanese character; on the walls, a picture of the Buddha, brush paintings of nature scenes. This room is homey but spare, a former living room turned into a gathering room where Sevan Sensei—a teacher's title goes after his or her name when the teacher is addressed—will talk to us a little about what to expect before we go upstairs to the newly refurbished zendo.

"The mind is a free-association machine," Ross explains. "You're never where you are, you're [mentally] elsewhere." We will be starting with what essentially are mechanical details about posture and breathing, but there is more to the practice and a reason for its mechanical details.

"We are a tradition of exploration," Ross explains. "To do deep exploration we need a form. Inside the discipline is enormous freedom. You're free when whatever you're doing is what you want."

After Ross completes his introduction, we head upstairs to the refurbished zendo. Some walls have been demolished, and the second-floor room is now more spacious, with bare expanses of golden-oak floor and quiet gray walls. On the sparely appointed altar in the room sits a small Buddha figure from China, positioned slightly above eye level and leading the eye upward. Before the Buddha are arranged various offerings, including candles, flowers, and fruit.

Jim, a senior student, greets us and instructs us in the basics of sitting meditation: how to position the legs, hands, eyes, head, shoulders, and trunk. All the senior students sitting with us beginners have beautifully erect postures. We are told how to position our cushions on the mat and how to sit to avoid unnecessary pain or strain. Jim mentions tricks for positioning weak knees or other recalcitrant limbs or joints and for avoiding pressure on the sciatic nerve, which can cause the leg to fall asleep. Zazen is strenuous but not sadistic. Then we are instructed in breath-counting up to ten, integrating silent counting with breathing. Finally, we are told something about the etiquette of group meditation: Don't move, rustle, or scratch an itch.

A zendo monitor, usually a senior student, and in this case, Jim, is in charge of keeping time for the sitting round and for opening and closing it. The monitor taps a bell at three short intervals, during which time students settle into position. With a peremptory slap of a wooden block, the meditation round begins.

To minimize distraction, Zen students face the wall and count their breaths during zazen. In this way, students symbolically turn their backs on the external world, instead exploring the internal world. (Photo: courtesy of Chicago Zen Center)

Facing the wall, eyes open but unfocused, we sit, sit, sit.

That's all. No more, no less. Time passes, thoughts pass, breath flows in and out, as through a gateway.

"This is it?" one Buddhist monk asks another, incredulous, in a cartoon from the *New Yorker* magazine that has amused Zen students and others in on the joke.

This *is* it. Just this and all this: the present, boundless, form-is-emptiness and emptiness-is-form moment. Only sitting. Sitting, which requires a high tolerance for boredom, a high degree of openness, and highly flexible legs. Zen is sitting—not thinking, not praying, not sleeping on the cushion, not regretting, not daydreaming, not planning tomorrow's day or replaying yesterday's conversations or childhood's emotional programming.

"The depth of this practice is fathomless," Ross tells us.

In *Zen Mind, Beginner's Mind*, Shunryu Suzuki tells us,

> While you are continuing this practice, week after week, year after year, your experience will become deeper and deeper.... Just practice *zazen* in a certain posture. Do not think about anything. Just remain on your cushion without expecting anything.

Nothing Special

Zen is the Japanese term for a traditional form of Buddhism that originated in India but evolved as it moved through China—the Chinese term is *ch'an*—Japan, Korea, and Vietnam. *Zen* literally means "meditation"; its aim is enlightenment *(satori)*, also often phrased as realizing the true nature of things, or Buddha nature, as Buddha himself did when he sat meditating under a bodhi tree in his native India 2,500 years ago. Zen is a disciplined trajectory to enlightenment that teaches a student to overcome habitual dualistic thinking. Zen works through mind to go beyond mind, beyond thinking, and well beyond words. Often it might seem to involve word play or Lewis Carroll–like logical nonsense: "form is emptiness" or "your head is a dragon, your tail is a snake" are meant to stimulate thought and challenge intellectual business as usual.

Zazen, sitting meditation, is one tool for working with the mind. With time and meditation—what Zen masters might call hard training—the mind will become "clear mind." Clear mind sees past attachment to emotions, conditions, and objects—a human condition that Buddhists believe is the cause of suffering *(dukkha)* or dissatisfaction. Buddhists also believe that this suffering can cease, and Buddhism is about teaching the way to the cessation of suffering. Zen Buddhism focuses on attachments—to thoughts, judgments, ideas, words, concepts, anything—in order to disrupt them, to bring about sudden shifts in how we see things. So Zen leads the student along the path of study and meditative practice, practice, practice to an understanding of the true nature of all existence.

The beginning student of Buddhism understandably can feel confused or intimidated. With roots in a number of different Eastern cultures, Buddhism brings foreign terminology and unfamiliar practices, 2,500 years' worth of scripture and commentary, and as much sectarian and cultural diversity as any of the other major world religions. Walking into any Buddhist center is a little like taking a quick trip to Asia. While the students may be American, they may not be chanting in English or dressed in Western-style clothes. Pictures, statues, and sacred objects vary by center and tradition within Buddhism, but the overall look of most centers is foreign to the average American eye. The Zen Buddhist aesthetic, dominated by simple motifs drawn from nature, is visually spare. While Zen has ritual and detail, it is bare-bones Buddhism, in keeping with its central understanding of emptiness and its unelaborate practice: just sit and sit and sit.

Like its aesthetic, the language of Zen is also distinctive. Zen throws away so many conceptual categories that it almost seems to require a tongue of its own—"Zen talk" about "big mind" or "Buddha nature." It erases a lot of conventional distinctions: "Don't make good or bad," Zen Master Seung Sahn likes to tell his students. Things conventionally thought of as opposites are not: Form is emptiness and emptiness is form, the Buddha says in the *Heart Sutra* teaching. Fittingly, because so many influential Zen teachers have come from Asian countries, the English they use is radically simple, making the manner of their speech consistent with Zen's revelation of simplicity. Suzuki says in *Zen Mind, Beginner's Mind* of the "power" of Zen, "Before you obtain it, it is something wonderful, but after you attain it, it is nothing special. It is just you yourself, nothing special."

The Zen practitioner, who is often also called a student because Zen is both study and practice, can sit alone at home daily, making it a relatively accessible practice for someone with no access to a local center. But all students say that group meditation enhances their practice, and that center-based retreats are indispensable to growth. Many students say their first retreat was a spiritual watershed that first illustrated for them how Zen works as a way of training mind and body. In Zen it's not uncommon for students of a particular teacher to travel great distances for retreats. Similarly, teachers may travel among centers within a particular school to teach and lead retreats.

Zen is one principal branch of the Buddhist-religion tree that gained exposure and adherents in the United States slowly throughout the last century. Over a long career, Japanese writer and lecturer D. T. Suzuki, a layperson, did much to plant seeds that grew in the latter half of the twentieth century, nurtured by the presence of Japanese monk-teachers in America who began to attract a cadre of students, among them writers of the 1950s "beat generation." A number of the earliest American students, among them Robert Aitken and Roshi Philip Kapleau (*roshi* is a title that designates an experienced teacher), wrote significant works and established Zen centers. The San Francisco Zen Center, one of the largest Buddhist communities outside Asia, was established in 1962 by the Japanese monk Shunryu Suzuki, the influential writer of *Zen Mind, Beginner's Mind.*

Zen Elements

Teachers are an important part of Zen, but they are not repositories of knowledge; a Zen student is expected to find his or her own way to the experience of enlightenment. Zen is experience—not knowledge, not ideas, not words, not concepts. Zen is direct experience—not someone else's experience or knowledge, not mediated experience or book-based knowledge. When I asked one student how much a practitioner can learn about Zen by reading books about it, the response was a kind laugh. The question is so common that it has a well-known answer. Reading about the Zen experience, I was told, is like eating a menu to experience food.

But a teacher is a guide—indeed, almost a goad—who teaches correct form and detail and challenges a student's practice. A teacher always poses questions. Instruction is face to face, and has a name: *dokusan,* or interview. A teacher keeps a student on his or her Zen toes, and is expected to correct errors, not necessarily in a personally empathetic style. A good relationship between teacher and student is one key to developing a solid practice. Teachers are also keepers of the flame; authority to teach is formally transmitted from a teacher to a student, and the line of transmission from a given respected teacher is called lineage.

Lineage gives a beginner an idea of what kinds of emphases or styles will be found at a center. Beginning students can know something about what to expect if they know who their teacher's teachers are. Lineage is also important because it is the very vehicle of Buddhism, which is at heart an oral tradition. It is a way of tracing authority and legitimacy back to the historical Buddha himself.

Centers are another important aspect of Zen. They are hubs of education and practice, places where short and long retreats are held. A long retreat, or *sesshin,* may last seven days or longer. Centers are a kind of lodestone, holding a teacher and his or her students and offering intensive opportunities for meditation and practice.

Just as Zen is a branch of Buddhism, Zen itself has a number of schools within it, and knowing a little bit about that can help a beginner in choosing a place to visit for instruction. Schools are usually associated either with teachers or techniques. Teachers are designated as belonging to a particular lineage, or succession, from a significant individual.

Zen can differ by country and culture, teacher, or emphasis. The principal Japanese schools are Rinzai and Soto. Soto Zen relies on zazen, sitting meditation, as the tool to attain enlightenment. Rinzai also uses koans. Koans are riddles or paradoxical statements, given to a student by a teacher, that seem invariably to defy commonly accepted logic in order to challenge a student to a new, deeper understanding that is beyond logic. Some centers will use one approach, the other, or integrate the two. The Korean Kwan Um school founded by Seung Sahn uses zazen and koans, known as *kong-an*s, the equivalent Korean word. The Chicago Zen Center, which teaches in the lineage of Roshi Philip Kapleau, Rochester Zen Center founder, is primarily Soto, but also uses koans. The Vietnamese monk and teacher Thich Nhat Hanh is a world-renowned leader within another Zen school, which is sometimes called after him and is also known as "engaged Buddhism" because of its special emphasis on social action and peace.

Schools of Zen: Same and Different

Different Zen schools differ on details in ritual and practice, with some practices specially evolved for America. Kwan Um has a Korean Zen master, but Kwan Um students in this country like to use English, Margaret explains. "We call a robe a 'robe,'" she says. "And the stick," she says, referring to the somewhat misunderstood stick used in Zen sitting to help students stay attentive, "is just a stick." (The "wake-up stick"—*kyosaku* is the Japanese term—is used by a designated person in a Zen sitting to strike acupressure points on the shoulders of a student who requests it. The stick helps call a student's mind back from wherever it may have wandered.)

There may be differences in sitting rules. Soto practitioners sit in rows facing the wall; Kwan Um students sit in rows facing one another. Kwan Um practice permits a student to leave the mat, after bowing, if a limb should fall asleep; most Zen centers do not permit that kind of movement. Form is important and part of the content of Zen, which teaches the paradoxical equivalence of form and emptiness.

At the Chicago Zen Center, students are more likely to hear traditional Japanese terms such as *zafu* (cushion) and *zabuton* (mat). "A zafu is a zafu," says Ross, making a Zen joke and a comment on the use of English at the same time. Beginners need to know that the sitting rules there are relatively demanding, and also to understand that facing discomfort is part of the growth of mind Zen promotes. At our introductory session, we beginners are told that a slight edge of discomfort will help practice, and that individual movement disturbs group practice. Ross also encourages us to ask for the stick, so we can understand its function through direct experience. He explains the form for requesting the stick: a sitter raises his or her folded hands overhead when the zendo monitor can be heard walking around, midway through a round of sitting. After the monitor applies the stick, the sitter expresses thanks by again raising folded hands.

Ross is right: the stick doesn't hurt, and like any abrupt and strong physical sensation, it immediately produces renewed clarity and focus, the mental equivalent of physically straightening the posture.

One of the students at the introductory session says she has come to learn meditation in order to relax. Zen does not promise to be the right meditation form for this. Ross knows through the experience of these sessions that some of these beginners will walk out the door and never return. "This place does not exist so that we can be calm," he tells the group of beginners, maybe warning some among us.

Margaret puts it bluntly: "Zen isn't for the faint-hearted."

Zen Stories

Margaret: "the answer that is not an answer"
While there is no substitute for the direct, personal experience of Zen, other people's stories of how they came to Zen, and how the practice fits in their lives, help ready the ground for direct experience. Margaret's story is an exemplary tale of years of spiritual journey that led, in a most unlikely way, to a Zen home.

Margaret began her spiritual journey in early adulthood, when, she says, "Lots of bad things happened and gave me what we call a 'big question.'" She expresses her "big question" as a question about suffering: Why does it happen? Margaret looked for the answer down a variety of paths, including psychology—today, she is a social worker—Christianity, twelve-step recovery, and no religion at all.

"For a long time," she explains, "I wanted an answer. But then I found it was never really the answer." Like many students, she read a great deal about Buddhism before beginning a practice. When she began, she practiced insight meditation, drawn from the Theravada branch of Buddhism, a different practice for focusing attention and developing greater awareness. She was at the point of seriously considering residential training at the Insight Meditation Society in Barre, Massachusetts, one of the most respected centers within the insight tradition, but, she says, "Instead, I went to graduate school." She obtained a master's degree in social work in 1990.

Although her academic immersion temporarily displaced her spiritual seeking and meditation practice, as her studies drew to a close, she encountered the Dances of Universal Peace, a spiritual practice originated by Samuel Lewis, an American Sufi (Islam's mystical branch). The Dances draw on music, chanting, and movement from a number of world spiritual traditions. "I really, really liked it immediately," says Margaret. "I've always been musical. I got involved in it and began to teach it." She was also active in a Christian peace church.

In 1992, she attended a conference about a variety of meditation traditions with the intention of learning more about insight meditation, not Zen. "The idea of getting hit with a stick didn't interest me," she says. Ironically, however, the Zen practice group and teacher she met were more conveniently located; the insight teacher came from another state. She also heard intimations of something as she listened to the Zen teacher, Barbara (Bobbie) Rhodes, one of Seung Sahn's first American students, who studied with him in Providence, Rhode Island, the location of Kwan Um's North American headquarters. Margaret found both teacher and teaching accessible—"We don't call her Bobbie *Soen Nim* [a Korean appellation of respect] or Zen Master Bobbie, just Bobbie"— and was intrigued enough by what she heard to do a three-day retreat.

"There was nothing that wasn't hard," she recalls. Mornings always began early, with 108 full bows. Sitting during retreats usually went on for ten hours or more. Meals were eaten in the formal Zen way, using four bowls that a person cleans with barley tea, which is then swallowed. Zen eating is a teaching tool, not a gourmet experience. "I didn't die," she says, "but I couldn't walk for three days afterward." Yet there was something compelling about her experience that drew her on.

"I think it was how clear I got, at least briefly, in that short a time," she says, "but I wasn't crazy about it, for a *long* time. I think I kept coming only because I have good karma."

Today, Margaret, with short gray hair, pale blue eyes, and lines of experience on her face, is sixty, and she loves the bowing and chanting that goes along with sitting. "I didn't start practicing till I was over fifty," she says. "To undertake Zen at fifty is not commonly done."

For Margaret, Zen is an answer that's—like a good Zen koan—not an answer. "My job," the social worker says, "has always been about suffering: 'Can you fix this?' Zen says, 'Not yes, not no. What is fixing?'"

"It feels," she continues, pausing, looking thoughtfully for words, "like Zen is a medicine I apply to the suffering in the world. That is what it's like to me: it's a way you hold that suffering."

Debby: "There are many different ways of finding your way"

Debby, another Kwan Um Zen student, describes herself as a practicing American Buddhist. She grew up in Indiana, which tends to yield corn, soybeans, and relatively conservative Christians. She had a patchwork Protestant upbringing, attending churches of different denominations. She also went with friends to a Catholic church.

"I was used to a potpourri and didn't get locked into the mindset of 'There is only one way,'" she explains. She also remembers liking mythology as a child and reading stories about Asian cultures and figures. So when she went to Anderson University in Indiana in the mid-1980s, taking a religious studies course was pretty logical. That introduced her to many religious traditions, Zen among them. "It had more resonance" than any of the others, she explains.

Finding information about Zen Buddhism in central Indiana was not easy. Debby remembers walking into a local bookstore that was part of a national chain. "They had two books on Buddhism, and I bought them both," she says. One was Philip Kapleau's *The Three Pillars of Zen;* the other was the Dhammapada, meaning "The Path of Teaching," a text of some basic teachings of the Buddha. Using Kapleau's book, Debby taught herself, even trying to sew some of the garments described in the book. She meditated privately at home.

"I didn't tell anybody," she says. She remembers conversations with her sister about religion and beliefs. "My sister was dumbfounded that I didn't have a central conviction that God existed," Debby says.

Practice got easier, or at least more public reinforcement, when Debby moved to California to take a high-tech job. After the cornfields of Indiana, she was in Elysian Fields for American Zen: the San Francisco Bay area, where practice centers are numerous and easy to find. She belonged for several years to Kannon Do at Mountain View, an affiliate of the San Francisco Zen Center. Then an abrupt job transfer brought Debby back to the Midwest, but this time to the suburban Chicago area. The closest Zen practice center was the suburban Kwan Um center.

She likens the differences between schools within Zen to differences in Christian denominations. "There are many different ways of finding your way," she says. "After a while, you get less stuck on the particulars."

Andy: "There's enough suffering already"

Like Debby, Andy, another Kwan Um Zen practitioner, came from Indiana, and also encountered world religions in college. "I came to the conclusion that what religion you would practice depended on where you were born," he says. He was born Episcopalian, but it didn't stick. In the early 1990s, his early exposures to Buddhism—he got "stuck with" and then fascinated by Buddhist sculpture as a research topic in high school—came back, and he found himself studying Tibetan Buddhism. He subsequently found himself growing skeptical of the considerable panoply of divine figures in Tibetan Buddhism and, at the same time, encountered a Kwan Um Zen teacher who led his way through both textual study and meditation. That worked, and he has practiced Zen for nine years.

Andy relies on Buddhism to help him do his work. An attorney who specializes in debt collection, he meets people whose difficult situations can prompt some pretty desperate behavior. "There's enough suffering already," Andy says. "You try to not add to it. There are situations where it's hard to practice Buddhism, but it helps. You don't lose your temper, you don't yell at them."

"It's impossible for me to tell if I'm growing up," says Andy, who is forty-eight, "or being transformed by Buddhism."

Sevan Ross: "Zen is about losing"

Sevan Ross says that he was raised a "nominal" Catholic in Pittsburgh. He found himself becoming the obnoxious kid in catechism class, the one who kept asking questions. "I would ask questions they couldn't give me satisfactory answers for, and then I would go out and play baseball," he recalls.

By the time he got to Indiana University of Pennsylvania, he was, as he describes it, "on spiritual hold." Then he took a class in world religions taught by a Chinese Presbyterian who was, Ross suspects, a Buddhist at heart. That struck him and stuck with him, and in the mid-1970s he found himself working as a schoolteacher in Syracuse, New York, near Rochester, where Roshi Philip Kapleau had opened the Rochester Zen Center in 1966, after thirteen years of Zen study in Japan. Ross went to the center. "Immediately I felt like I found home," he recalls. "At the first chanting service I cried like a baby."

For Ross, Zen is the forum for spiritual exploration that he had been seeking, a forum that is independent of a set of beliefs that has a God, a hierarchy, and spiritual dogma. "I wanted to go deeply into the essence of things without the impingement of a God," he explains. "Zen is an environment of exploration. Suddenly the responsibility was mine. No one was preaching beliefs at me."

In 1981 he moved to Rochester to be able to study at the center. To

Zen priest and teacher Sensei Sevan Ross is dressed in his robes. He holds a kotsu, *a symbol of his teaching authority. Within Zen, a formal ceremony marks the transmission of authority to teach. (Photo: Joseph Sorrentino)*

do so, he changed jobs, becoming a corporate recruiter. Although head-hunter and Zen student might at first blush seem antithetical, he tried to see his job as Buddhist "right livelihood"—work performed ethically in a way that did not harm. "I had clients come to me because they considered me honest," he says.

Eventually, a shift in his own priorities in the late 1980s prompted him to ask to join the staff at the Rochester center. He thought the job would last a year. "I caught the bug," he says. "It was clear to me that working with the dharma [Buddhist teachings] daily was where I wanted to be."

So he worked on the staff for eight years and was ordained a priest in 1992, signifying his commitment to working at a Buddhist temple. He came to the Chicago Zen Center in 1996 and was sanctioned as a teacher—made a *sensei*—in 1998. The Chicago center had been an affiliate of the Rochester center, but the sanctioning of Ross made the Chicago center formally independent within a larger association of centers all related to the lineage of Kapleau.

Ross likes to say that Zen offers nothing. "What can you gain? Nothing. Zen is about losing—losing encrustations, beliefs, opinions, the need to have opinions."

Jim: "The work is entirely yours to do"

Like so many students approaching Buddhism or another culturally unfamiliar religion, Jim, the senior student at the Chicago Zen Center who gave me instruction on posture and breathing, began by reading. He read lots of different books on Zen, and instead of increased clarity, he simply felt confusion at how cryptic they were. "That confusion, more than anything else, drove me to actual practice," he says. "I've never gone back to books much."

He's been practicing since 1990, when he and his wife moved from Paris so that Jim could take a job as a chocolate chef at a well-known French restaurant in suburban Chicago. At the time, the Chicago center had no resident teacher, and was considered a satellite facility of the Rochester center. At its core were serious students who were highly self-motivated. "That says something about their personal commitment," Jim says. "People who are there on a 'tourist' level aren't going to hang around that kind of environment."

Still, Jim remembers early on in his practice wanting the guidance of a teacher and convincing himself that enlightenment would happen faster or the way it was described in the books he had read if only he had a teacher. "I craved teacher contact in the beginning, thinking there would be something magical," he recalls. "You're expecting a guru. Yet the best teachers will tell you up front: The work is entirely yours to do."

Sung: "I kind of lucked into it"

Sung, a Korean American student at the Chicago Zen Center, had Buddhist grandparents and remembers going to a Buddhist temple when he was young. Otherwise, he had "an atheistic kind of background" growing up, laced with spiritual curiosity.

"I always had these nagging questions when I was little, nagging metaphysical questions, like 'What am I doing here?' I got into studying astronomy when I was little, but that didn't satisfy me."

When he arrived at the University of Chicago in 1978 for undergraduate study, one of the first things he found was a spiritual path. He made friends with a student from Colorado who was studying Tibetan Buddhism. His friend's explanations were sufficiently intriguing to prompt Sung to begin searching the Chicago phone book for Buddhist centers. He was also reading, and like so many others, found Kapleau's book. Then he found the Chicago Zen Center, at that time an affiliate of the Rochester Zen Center. He even found someone who was driving forty miles from Chicago's south to north sides on weekends so that he could get easily to the Zen Center.

"I kind of lucked into it," he says now.

It wasn't luck that prompted him to persist, however. His nagging metaphysical questions are still there, but, "After all these years I feel I'm getting closer to the truth," says Sung, who is now forty and a trader at the Chicago Board of Trade, an occupation that gives him enough free time to go on Zen retreats.

Elie: "I never thought it would be so simple"

Elie, a school and clinical psychologist, is another student at the Chicago Zen Center. His journey to Zen began in a small village in the biblical area of Galilee in what is now Israel. He was an Arab in Israel who was raised as a Christian. He spent most of his childhood in Catholic orphanages, where the priests and nuns, mostly Europeans, treated him very well and inculcated in him a ritual Catholicism that remains imprinted on him today. As a young boy, he would occasionally serve as an altar boy, an assistant to the priest officiating at the Catholic Mass.

"These were indescribable moments—the incense, the smell of wine, images of Bible," Elie, who is now fifty-one, says. "I sometimes say to people who ask me, 'When I was a small boy I could see, smell, feel, and taste God, and I loved it.'"

But doctrine and dogma were distinctly less appealing to him, and his youthful religious zeal waned, although his beliefs were not extinguished. Then, while studying psychology in Chicago as a young adult, he grew interested in the work of Carl Jung and Jung's ideas about archetypes—universal symbols and stories that recur in human culture and also inform individual psychological development. Through Jung's work, the meaning of Jesus and the central ideas of Christianity changed for Elie.

"All the archetypal ideas that make up Christianity became relative and easy to shake," he says. And so he continued his spiritual search with this newer perspective, still pursuing fundamental spiritual questions, but with growing certainty that their answers did not lie outside the human mind or somewhere in the sky. He explored Tibetan Buddhism a little, but found it too reminiscent of Catholicism. Then a fellow Jungian analyst and friend, who was returning to his homeland of India, gave Elie a box of books.

Elie remembers taking one book after another out of the box and laying them aside. "I was not interested in anything that relies on form," Elie explains. "I wanted to search for something that goes beyond form in a way. The truth cannot be something other than that, or it cannot be only the specific form of Catholicism or Hinduism. All of these are part of the diversity of the totality that is one." The last book in the box was Kapleau's *The Three Pillars of Zen*. He opened it and began reading.

"I put it down eight hours later, " he says. "I must have read the whole thing in one sitting." He had found the path he was seeking, and was eager to go down it and began sitting. Eventually, he began to search for centers in the Chicago area. At the first one he called, the abbot talked to him for an hour. He crossed that place off his list. Then he called the Chicago Zen Center and learned they practiced in the Kapleau lineage. He began going there in the late 1980s, and has been studying Zen since then.

Zen ostensibly offers nothing, but Elie finds it eminently practical in his life and work. "We all live for tomorrow, we all live for a dream, for sometime in the future, whether we dream of retiring next year or at sixty-five," he begins. "We look at our work as a burden, we fight traffic, we have a daily routine and hassle and pettiness, all those struggles of daily life, and we want to escape that. I don't feel that anymore."

When he first came to Zen, Elie felt differently, and he had no idea what would happen through Zen practice. "I had no clue," he says, slowly and deliberately, underlining his words. "I never thought it would be so simple and so clean and so transparent. And so vast."

Steps for Beginners

- Read some books. They will give you little tastes of the world that Zen opens to the meditator. Zen has been a serious practice in America long enough for books to be written by teachers who understand the contemporary American context for Zen practice. The majority of students start by reading, looking for something that will catch their attention. Don't be misled, however, into thinking that reading about Zen is doing Zen. Zen teachers say that teaching about Zen is the finger pointing at the moon, and like to admonish students not to mistake the finger for the moon. Zen emphasizes experience; Zen *is* experience.

- If possible, visit centers. This will give you an idea of who goes there and will give you some immediate sense of whether you're comfortable or not.

■ Assess the teacher. This can be a little tricky. One experienced Buddhist I know remarked that whichever teacher is in front of you is the one you love. Over the course of its establishment in this country, and translation of its Asian-derived mores to American mores, Buddhism has occasionally faced problems with teachers' ethics and behavior. Some initial objectivity can be helpful and prudent.

The opposite reaction—dislike—may be worth examining, too. Some students say that they ultimately benefited greatly from teachers whom they did not necessarily like as individuals. Like the finger pointing at the moon, a teacher is the instrument conveying the teaching. It can be helpful to reflect on the reasons for your response to a particular environment or teacher. A needed challenge isn't always attractive.

■ Sit regularly. Then sit some more. Many teachers tell students to sit five minutes longer than they think they can. There are no shortcuts or ten-minute paths to enlightenment. Elie, a student of Zen for a dozen years, told me with sympathetic glee, "You have to do the work."

Selected Resources

Books

Aitken, Robert. *Taking the Path of Zen.* San Francisco: North Point Press, 1982.

Kapleau, Philip. *The Three Pillars of Zen.* Garden City, N.Y.: Anchor/ Doubleday, 1980.

Maguire, Jack. *Waking Up: A Week Inside a Zen Monastery.* Woodstock, Vt.: SkyLight Paths, 2000.

Mitchell, Stephen, ed. *Dropping Ashes on the Buddha: The Teachings of Zen Master Seung Sahn.* New York: Grove Press, 1976.

Nhat Hanh, Thich. *The Miracle of Mindfulness: A Manual of Meditation.* Boston: Beacon Press, 1975.

Suzuki, Shunryu. *Zen Mind, Beginner's Mind.* New York: Weatherhill, 1970.

Centers and organizations

Providence Zen Center
99 Pound Road
Cumberland, RI 02864
919-967-0861
www.kwanumzen.org

Rochester Zen Center
7 Arnold Park
Rochester, NY 14607
716-473-9180
www.rzc.org

San Francisco Zen Center
300 Page Street
San Francisco, CA 94102
415-863-3136
www.sfzc.com

Zen Center of Los Angeles
923 South Normandie Avenue
Los Angeles, CA 90006-1301
213-387-2351
www.zencenter.com

Zen Mountain Monastery
P.O. Box 197
South Plank Road
Mt. Tremper, NY 12457
845-688-2228
www.mro.org/zmm/zmm.shtml

Internet sites

- www.buddhanet.net—A "Gateway to Buddhism" (all traditions).

- www.ciolek.com/WWWVL-Zen.html—An admirable online library for Zen Buddhism.

- www.dharmanet.org/infowebz.html—A listing of online Zen centers and other resources.

- www.parallax.org—The Unified Buddhist Church, the U.S. organization for the work of Vietnamese Zen Buddhist monk Thich Nhat Hanh, with valuable links to related centers and organizations.

3

Insight Meditation: Being Mindful

Mindfulness means paying attention in a particular way: on purpose, in the present moment, and nonjudgmentally. This kind of attention nurtures greater awareness, clarity, and acceptance of present-moment reality.

JON KABAT-ZINN, *WHEREVER YOU GO, THERE YOU ARE: MINDFULNESS MEDITATION IN EVERYDAY LIFE*

Only Breathing

On a sunny and mild May afternoon, the wind is ruffling the freshly unfurled spring leaves on maple and ash trees. The crewcut-trim grass is firm underfoot. Perched on cushions parked on rubber mats atop the terrain, ten people meditate in the shade of the trees. In the distance across a sloping green field, a blue-and-white-striped awning signals that a small party is taking place at a neighboring house.

I'm one of the group sitting silently under the trees, just as Buddha sat beneath the bodhi tree, a kind of fig, in his native India 2,500 years ago, vowing not to get up until he had attained enlightenment. Six years of searching had led the Buddha to a May night under a full moon. Toward dawn, truth began to dawn—the Four Noble Truths: There is suffering in the world; suffering has a cause; suffering has an end; and a path exists to end suffering. Craving, ignorance, and hatred—the sources of human suffering—dropped from the Buddha like blinders and he realized enlightenment.

Those of us gathered at the Buddhadharma Meditation Center to follow the Buddha's path are neither so fortunate nor so well disciplined; enlightenment is more of a lifetime project than a realistic goal for our one-day insight meditation retreat. Still, we are practicing; we are practicing by doing something we knew how to do as soon as we were born.

We are breathing: in, out, in, out. We are paying attention to our breathing as a way of increasing our awareness of what we do. That is all we are doing: breathing and observing our breathing. Whenever our attention is drawn away from the activity of breathing, we are to look briefly at what has claimed our attention—a thought, a distracting sound—and label it accordingly: *Thinking. Hearing.* Then, we are to let the thought go, and return our attention to what we are doing: simply breathing, in and out.

Breathing may be an instinctive action since birth, but doing it consciously and paying close and exclusive attention to it is far harder than it sounds. Breathing even becomes a little challenging when it is all I am supposed to be doing. With a lot of ordinary external distraction swept away, I feel like two people: one breathing, one watching.

Buddha taught that humans have six senses: the five conventional senses of sight, hearing, taste, touch, and smell, and the sixth sense of the mind, which perceives mental objects. Even when sensory stimulation is minimal, the mind can, and usually does, remain very busy, by its very nature. Thoughts rush in to fill the mind's vacuum.

The daylong retreat involves more than sitting meditation. After thirty minutes of sitting, our teacher and meditation leader, Ajahn Sompoch, strikes a bell, and his deliberate gesture produces a low metallic hum. *Ajahn*—a title of respect for a Thai monk—Sompoch is a Thai man perhaps in his thirties, head shaven, bespectacled, dressed in traditional monastic orange robes.

The bell signals us to begin walking meditation. We walk, even though we are going nowhere. We do not form a line, but each person marks out a small, individual route, circumambulating silently. Walking, I find a path in the middle of the grass that I seem to stick to without even trying. I try to be mindful of only what I am doing, just lifting, moving, and putting down my feet, one by one, left, right, left, right, lifting, moving, putting down.

The simple task of walking feels slightly foreign, just as breathing has felt unfamiliar. I sometimes feel wobbly or off balance. I try to picture myself making contact with the earth, but that visualization is itself somewhat distracting. Ajahn Sompoch suggests later that I may be walking too slowly, or maybe trying too hard to "get it right," a common affliction of beginners. The alternation of two activities is nice. Walking offers relief for legs that have been folded up for sitting meditation; in turn, sitting helps to slow my thought stream down, in ever so tiny increments, each time we return to our cushions.

We began this daylong retreat at nine o'clock in the morning with chanting in Pali, one of the historic languages of Buddhism, and a *dhamma* (teaching) talk, during which Ajahn Sompoch tells us a little about right view or right understanding, the first step of the eightfold path the Buddha taught that leads to the overcoming of suffering. Each step of the path—right view, right intention, right speech, right action, right livelihood, right effort, right mindfulness, and right concentration—is distinct, but ultimately, like all things Buddhist, its steps are interconnected. Our meditation practice during the day will help us toward right understanding by giving us a little experience of how things arise and pass away, a key element of Buddhist teaching.

For the day, then, we alternate half-hour sitting and walking meditation, with a ninety-minute break for lunch. The food is as good as that found in any Thai restaurant, only it's homemade; there is also American-style food.

Two monks, our teacher and another resident monk, eat first. After the monks select their food, they sit down with it on raised platforms off to one side of the dining room. Then two students step forward to offer the food to the monks, holding out to them a plate and cup. This is part of the Theravada Buddhist tradition; the rules by which monks live require them to accept food as a gift. The ritual offering of food fulfills this requirement.

The American meditation students eat at the table, with one notable change from a normal meal: we eat in silence. We do this in order to maintain the spirit of mindfulness throughout the day. After lunch we can walk the ten-acre grounds, where the center has been located since 1988. Underlining the growing presence of world religions in America, a white-walled mosque is rising on the site right next door to the Buddhist center.

The center itself stretches back from a busy suburban highway. A triangular sign with the center's name in Thai and English, topped by a carving of a lotus, greets the visitor turning in. The lotus is ubiquitous in Buddhism; the flowering water plant, rooted in mud but open to the sun, symbolizes enlightenment. Lotuses carved in stone also stand atop pedestals in front of the sand-colored brick temple building. Potted plants and landscaping lend a tropical touch to the entrance area.

A wagon wheel near the entrance sign is at first a puzzling object. But this American-looking artifact, found on the property, fits in nicely with the central Buddhist metaphor of the wheel. Eight-spoked wheels— symbolizing the eightfold path—are common symbols in Buddhism.

Behind the temple, which also holds a banquet hall for community functions, the grounds extend back. The temple building cuts off the sounds of traffic whizzing past, making for quiet acreage where we can meditate outdoors.

The group meditation resumes at one o'clock with time for questions and answers before we go back to alternating periods of sitting and walking. Through the afternoon, the sun slowly slides across the spring sky, changing the shadows cast by the trees. We then adjourn to the temple for a closing discussion period. Ajahn Sompoch asks each participant to report or comment on the day's practice, and in turn offers some comments to individual students. This is *dhamma* group discussion. One student says he was preoccupied by a personal difficulty; the monk comments that the student seemed to be moving exceptionally quickly during walking meditation. After this kind of exchange, we close the day by again chanting in Pali.

Phra Sunthorn Plamintr, seated on the dais, was the founding abbot of Buddhadharma Meditation Center. Buddhadharma, like some insight meditation centers, serves the needs of ethnic Buddhists as well as American converts. Other insight meditation centers teach a more Americanized form of insight meditation practice, emphasizing meditation and dispensing with much of the ritual Buddhist context from which it comes. (Photo: courtesy of Buddhadharma Meditation Center)

My own insight after a full-day insight meditation retreat was how difficult it was for me to pay attention, to sit, to breathe, to walk, to be mindful. My mind kept getting up from the cushion, going backward into the past, skipping forward into the future, going next door to the party—going any place but here, visiting any time but now. Listening to others' comments, I learned that I did not have the only busy mind in the group. Others remarked about their sleepy limbs, mental distractions, and difficulties in sustaining pure attention.

Practice, and More Practice

In the insight meditation tradition, meditation is all about learning to pay attention. Learning implies that whatever we set out to learn is something we don't know. Paying full, systematic, undivided attention is a skill to learn, and so it requires practice: repeated doing. Meditation provides that, meditation is that: practice, an activity undertaken repeatedly in order to see clearly, to attain insight into the nature of reality. The way the mind works in perceiving reality has a lot to do with determining that reality. Insight meditation offers understanding of how the mind works. It is a tool the Buddha himself used to attain enlightenment. The Buddha sat beneath the bodhi tree until he discovered the Four Noble Truths: suffering, the cause of suffering, the cessation of suffering, and the path to ending suffering. Insight shows us that our mind creates suffering.

Insight meditation is also commonly called *vipassana*, a Pali term that means "insight." "*Vipassana* means to see things, see characteristics of things as they really are. People never look to see themselves, they never look within," says Ajahn Chuen Phangcham, a respected senior monk and teacher in this tradition. "When you go to meditate you need to look within, and then you see your mind, you observe your mind; then you train your mind and see the way of its working."

Walking meditation. Meditation is not just sitting; mindfulness is also practiced through walking in a deliberate and attentive manner. Walking meditation is another way of training the mind to pay attention. (Photo: courtesy of Buddhadharma Meditation Center)

In *A Path with Heart: A Guide through the Perils and Promises of Spiritual Life,* insight meditation teacher Jack Kornfield memorably compares learning how to meditate with training a puppy.

> You put the puppy down and say "stay." Does the puppy listen? It gets up and it runs away. You sit the puppy back down again and say "stay." And the puppy runs away over and over again.

So it is with insight meditation, which teaches the meditator through repeated practice of observing the mind at work. Over time and with training, we can begin to see things as they really are. We will gain insight.

An Evolving Tradition

Buddhism is a tapestry of beliefs and practices, and over its 2,500-year history this major world religion has adapted as it has crossed national and cultural boundaries, evolving a number of different cultural identities and expressions. Insight meditation as it's most frequently taught in this country comes from Thailand and other Southeast Asian countries, from the Buddhist tradition known as Theravada, which means "teaching of the elders of the order." Insight meditation is sometimes taught within an ethnic Asian Buddhist context, as at Buddhadharma, and sometimes as a kind of stand-alone practice, apart from the ritual and devotional practices of a religion. Kornfield and colleagues Joseph Goldstein and Sharon Salzberg all studied in Thailand or Burma, then went on to establish the Insight Meditation Society in Barre, Massachusetts, in 1976. A sibling center, Spirit Rock Meditation Center, organized by Kornfield and others in the San Francisco Bay area, evolved in the early 1980s. Kornfield deliberately minimized some aspects of the Buddhist religion in order to make the teaching of insight meditation more immediately accessible to Americans. These two centers are hubs for the intensive practice of American-style insight meditation. Spirit Rock is also a principal center for teacher training.

So although they are both teaching in the Theravada tradition, Asian and American teachers of meditation may differ in their interpretations and emphases. For example, little teaching is done in the American insight tradition about the cycles of rebirth that are a part of Asian Theravada Buddhism's beliefs about reality. Many American insight meditation teachers and practitioners generally regard meditation practice as the primary expression of Theravada Buddhist spirituality, and they present the teachings in a psychological framework that seems quintessentially American and more consistent with prevailing American cultural assumptions about reality and more grounded in familiar experience.

Another difference is that American insight meditation is highly accessible and practical for laypeople, compared to its monastic Asian roots. The earliest teachers of key American practitioners were Asian monks, but American insight meditation is preeminently a practice for people who hold jobs, raise families, and live in the everyday world rather than in a monastery. This type of Buddhism as laypeople practice it is also sometimes known as "householder Buddhism."

Buddhadharma Meditation Center tries to bridge the lay and religious worlds, the American and the immigrant. It has a monastic function—the center is home for a community of half a dozen monks—and it also serves laypeople, both ethnic Thai and American. Offering language classes and Sunday school for the young, it serves Thai members with cultural concerns; it also attracts adult Americans who are interested in insight meditation practice. It regularly holds retreats and classes on meditation and Buddhist teaching.

Buddhadharma is noticeably bicultural. The signs in the temple are in Thai and English; the chant books, with prayers and chants, contain three languages, Thai, Pali, and English. Sunday services alternate languages: the first, third, and fifth Sunday in English, the second and fourth in Thai. The orange-robed monks are Thai, except for Ven. (for "Venerable," a title) Nyanasobhano, who, despite his Thai name, is an American, thin, bespectacled, and distinctly taller than his Thai counterparts. The American monk leads meditation instruction classes weekly; virtually all his students are American. Attendance averages eight to ten at the classes.

Buddhadharma promotes the teachings of the Thai monk Buddhadasa Bhikku, who wrote *Mindfulness with Breathing: A Manual for Serious Beginners* (Wisdom, 1996). The center takes part in the Buddhadasa for World Peace project by disseminating the teacher's work. Buddhadasa Bhikku, who died in 1993, is considered one of the most influential contemporary Thai teachers of Buddhism. He taught *anapanasati*, a type of meditation on the breath.

The center, located in a former Baptist church that has been transformed into a temple, retains something of the look of its earlier use. The meditation hall is like a church of the Buddha. A huge golden statue of the Buddha, illuminated by indoor spotlights, sits up front where a baptistery had been. The room has pews, although there is also a large open area where students can sit on meditation cushions. Meditation instruction takes place here weekly, in the form of a short presentation followed by a forty-minute practice period.

Where to Practice

Serious practitioners with financial resources can travel to centers—such as Insight Meditation Society (IMS), Spirit Rock, and Buddhadharma—that regularly offer retreats. Another way of practicing and learning is through local sitting groups, which are informally organized and constitute a large network. There are at least 250 insight meditation sitting groups convening throughout the country, according to listings of teacher-led and sitting groups published in early 2001 in *Inquiring Mind,* a twice-yearly journal of the *vipassana* community. But major centers have also extended their influence and teaching through books, cassette tapes, and videos that, in effect, can offer some instruction where centers do not exist. In addition, other teachers have contributed to the growth and development of the insight tradition in America, among them the Indian S. N. Goenka, the American Ruth Denison, and Henepola Gunaratana, a Sri Lankan.

Stories from Practitioners at Buddhadharma

Eric: "It's more than just meditation"
Eric, thirty-six, has been practicing and studying insight meditation at Buddhadharma for three years. Raised in no specific religious tradition,

he has always been interested in philosophy and religion, reading widely and studying. "I came to the realization you have to meditate in order to develop spiritually," he explains. "Reading is just two-dimensional, and you have to *do* something to facilitate truth."

Interested in meditation, Eric took a class at a community college. That class included field trips, and one of them brought him to Buddhadharma. There he heard a talk from the American monk Ajahn Nyanasobhano.

"I thought, 'Wow.' I really liked his lucid, scientific style, the way he approached meditation," Eric says. "It appealed to me—no mysticism, just 'Hey, this is how you do it.' I started going there and have been going back ever since."

Eric, who works in computer technology, has done a number of retreats, including some four-day sessions, and he works on maintaining a daily practice as well as attending weekly group meditation and Buddhist study. He has introduced friends to it, and they find it makes sense, he says.

He considers himself an American Buddhist. Buddhism makes sense to him because he finds it eminently practical and different from the "God-in-the-sky" style of Western religions. "It's not about belief; belief isn't going to take you there, you've got to practice," Eric says. "I got attracted because of the meditation, and I see now, 'Ah, it's more than just meditation.'"

Sonny: "This is the best way for me"

Sonny is an ethnic Indian interested in Buddhism. He is also a Jain. He doesn't find the two religions mutually exclusive. "I don't believe in labels," he explains. "I'm not being a Jain *or* Buddhist. If I learn about religion through Buddhism, it doesn't make me any less a Jain."

Sonny, thirty-two, is an engineer who was born in America but raised in India. He wants to be active in his local Jain community, but he also

wants to pursue his interest in Buddhism. He is fairly new to the Buddhadharma center, having only come for a month. He had been meditating on his own for two years and read some books, but felt he lacked
guidance.

Sonny tackled a one-day retreat early in his practice and learned
something. "It gave me a good idea of the way I should be practicing,"
he says ruefully. "It got me in tune with my shortcomings. I found out
how impatient I really am."

He plans to continue attending group meditation sessions and to
develop his practice. "This is the best way for me," he says.

Diana: "The Buddha wasn't a god"

Diana, another meditator, travels forty-five minutes to Buddhadharma
from her home in another suburb. She first encountered meditation more
than two years ago, when a course based on work done by Jon Kabat-
Zinn was offered in her workplace. Kabat-Zinn has applied principles of
insight meditation—he uses the term "mindfulness" to describe the meditation he teaches—in developing a clinical program for stress manage-
ment, called mindfulness-based stress reduction. In an essay in *The Faces
of Buddhism in America* (University of California Press, 1998), insight
meditation teacher and scholar Gil Fronsdal calls Kabat-Zinn's work a
"'disguised' introduction of *vipassana* practice into American society."

After the course concluded, Diana maintained an interest, began
reading, started calling centers, and found Buddhadharma. "I came to
the Thursday night teaching class and it just sort of clicked," she says.
"It's a nice environment and the people were friendly. I felt it was a good
place."

The stress reduction course she took was a needed introduction to
the mind-body realm. Her initial interest in meditation was prompted
by health problems. "I'd be talking to somebody and I would be grab-
bing the wall because I was so dizzy," she explains. She experienced high

blood pressure and cardiac arrhythmias. It took six doctors to arrive at a diagnosis: panic attacks. "So that's how I came to meditation," she says. "A lot of scary health things and they couldn't find a cause."

Diana, forty-six, also does yoga, another mind-body discipline she was introduced to through the Kabat-Zinn course. She is taking courses in it. "Nothing tremendously elaborate," she says. "I just like to do it when I'm in a long meditative thing. I found it really helps me."

Like Eric, she now considers herself a Buddhist, though she was raised a Catholic. She left her faith as a young adult. "I didn't believe there was anyone there, any being, any entity, watching me," she explains. "I just couldn't see it." By contrast, Buddhism strikes her as less belief-oriented and more experience-based. "I looked and it made sense," she adds. "The Buddha wasn't a god; he was born and lived and died."

Diana has done a four-day insight meditation retreat, and found it tremendously challenging. "By the end, my back was hurting. I started crying in some of the meditation sessions. Lots of emotional stuff started coming up."

She also had a remarkable coda of an experience immediately after the retreat. A former professional musician, she had promised to attend a benefit concert. Although she was drained from the retreat, she was also determined to keep her promise to a friend. The concert was a revelation to her ears and being. "It was like I had never heard music before," she explains. "There was a way of listening to music with my whole being that I had never known."

Despite the difficulty of her previous experience, she is planning to do a ten-day retreat out of state led by teachers Joseph Goldstein and Steve Armstrong. "It's what I feel I need to do."

Dale: "Meditation is not particularly glamorous"
Dale has been meditating at Buddhadharma for three years. He is more comfortable sharing his views than his life story, but says he was raised

"hard-core Protestant Calvinist," a faith he hasn't followed since he was eighteen. Now a fifty-one-year-old chiropractor, he tries to take a realistic approach to his meditation practice. "I deeply understand that this is a long-term training procedure," he says. "It is not 'Can I feel good tonight?' Because this is a long-term training program, the worst part is the beginning. That's what stops a lot of people."

He's very emphatic that meditation is work, and people coming to it should appreciate that. "Meditation is not particularly glamorous, in my opinion," he says. "It takes a great deal of maturity and accurate expectations."

Stories from Practitioners at IMS and Spirit Rock

Other meditators who are insight practitioners identify themselves with the American insight meditation movement anchored by the Insight Meditation Society (IMS) and Spirit Rock centers. These practitioners are far more likely to use the term *vipassana*, the Pali term that means "insight," when describing their meditation practice; they tend to refer to themselves as the *vipassana* community. Many of them have done retreats at one of those centers, or work with teachers who have trained at or are associated with the centers. Their practice focuses on meditation and the Buddha's teachings about the nature of mind, making it a very psychological understanding and application of Buddhism.

Chris: "bridging the realms of mind and spirit"
Chris is a *vipassana* practitioner and teacher as well as a psychotherapist. He has done retreats at Spirit Rock and also taken training from Kabat-Zinn. His meditation practice began when he was in the Roman Catholic Jesuit novitiate in the 1980s. His adviser gave him a book about meditation, and that started his exploration of the relationship between psy-

chology and spirituality. He eventually left the Jesuits and instead earned a Ph.D. in counseling psychology.

His work with clients today bridges the realms of mind and spirit. He teaches mindfulness meditation to help clients in therapy. He also teaches it in workshops for those especially interested in the stress-reduction function of mindfulness meditation.

For him, meditation is a spiritual path. "If it's not that, it's not much of anything," Chris says.

Scott: "getting a better sense of how my mind works"

Scott, a Chicago resident, has studied at IMS via a correspondence course. He purchased tapes with a set of guided meditations and talks, and corresponded with a teacher by letter and e-mail.

"I liked it," he says. "I'm a relatively disciplined person." He undertook the tape training at the recommendation of a friend, and he has recommended it to others. Scott found the access to a teacher an especially valuable part of his long-distance study. "When you're practicing, things come up," he says. "It's good to have someone to talk to."

Scott, a thirty-two-year-old social worker who has been doing insight meditation for three and a half years, came to his practice via the work of Kabat-Zinn, just as Diana did. Scott heard about Kabat-Zinn's stress reduction program at the University of Massachusetts on a PBS television series hosted by journalist Bill Moyers. "It really spoke to me," says Scott. He had already been reading in world religions and mythology, and was struck by the work of Joseph Campbell, who brought Jungian psychological insight to the study of world religions. "Joseph Campbell was the one who really began to open my eyes to other traditions," Scott says. Scott had been raised in a Protestant tradition that taught him, he says, "'The Protestant tradition is *the* path to God.' That rigidity was something I couldn't live under once I got out on my own."

Scott now sits with Insight Chicago, a Chicago sitting group, or *sangha* (community), that gathers every other week for group meditation and has connections to IMS. Last summer he went on a thirty-day silent retreat at the Forest Way Insight Meditation Center in Ruckersville, Virginia, where he worked with meditation teacher and author Matthew Flickstein.

"I don't know in retrospect that I experienced profound changes between the beginning and end of retreat," says Scott. "I didn't find it extremely difficult. One of the big things that came out of the retreat was a better sense of how my mind works and the source of traps and potholes my mind gets stuck in and how to begin to work with those things."

Sandra: "My mind just opened up"

Insight Chicago is led by teacher Sandra Hammond, and is part of a Midwest network that also includes groups in Urbana, Illinois; Lafayette, Indiana; and the southern Chicago community of Matteson. "We don't have a meditation center per se, but we have the Prairie Sangha network," explains Hammond. "It feels like mitosis, like cellular division— an organism that's forming."

Those interested can receive instruction in insight meditation and have regular opportunity to practice group meditation. The group sittings are regularly scheduled and all home-based. Though they are not formal communities or centers, these *sangha*s all offer mentoring and annual retreats, and also have a process for doing business.

Trained by teachers at Spirit Rock and IMS, Hammond is authorized to teach and develop insight groups as a community dharma (teaching) leader; her guiding teachers are at IMS and Spirit Rock, and teachers from those centers lead Prairie Sangha extended retreats. In addition to its IMS-style core meditation practice, Prairie Sangha also uses the teachings of Tsoknyi Rinpoche, a Tibetan Buddhist teacher who heads the Pundarika Foundation in Nepal and has written *Carefree Dignity*

(Rangjung Yeshe Publications, 1998). Some cross-fertilization between the two traditions is exciting, Hammond believes, and portends more Buddhist spiritual resources for the Midwest area. But she is careful to distinguish among the teachings and influences.

"We practice insight meditation in exactly the traditional formal way," she says. "I'm very careful to point out what is the traditional way, and what comes from the Tibetan side of things."

Her own interest in insight meditation developed out of personal inclination and professional work. Hammond, fifty-eight, is a psychotherapist and teacher of psychotherapy who was involved in the Chicago-area development of family therapy. Her understanding of the process of interior life turned out to be very close to ideas of mental process and reality taught in insight meditation.

"My work in psychotherapy was pointing toward this understanding that the *buddhadharma* [Buddha's teaching] is about the mind," she says, "about how to understand the nature of mind and understand the nature of the afflictions of mind and how we can be free of them."

It was while working with a friend and fellow therapist that she began insight meditation in the early 1980s. "One day he said to me, 'Sandra, come and sit with me in the desert,'" she recalls. This invitation to a ten-day retreat opened doors and vistas for her.

"My mind just opened up; it was like coming home. And not only that, but I realized, 'This is what my work is about,'" she recalls. "It was personally coming home and, professionally, it made sense."

Prairie Sangha offers what Hammond believes is unique: a Committed Practice Conscious Living program, a yearlong intensive study and practice "for people who want to take time to bring forward into their lives a focus on their practice, formally and in their daily lives." The program contains lots of retreat time, time for teaching and "dharma buddies"—people who will support and reinforce the disciplined study and practice of insight meditation as a way of life.

Lovingkindness and Generosity

In addition to basic insight meditation, *vipassana* meditators make other meditative practices an important part of what they do. One of the practices especially popular with Americans is lovingkindness, also called *metta*, the Pali term for this quality. Lovingkindness cultivates compassion and open-mindedness and a realization of interconnectedness, a principal Buddhist teaching. A lovingkindness meditator concentrates the mind on phrases that express and foster compassion toward oneself and others, beginning with friends and benefactors and eventually moving on to those with whom one has difficulty or feels enmity toward. Like meditation, *metta* practice is done regularly, and *metta* retreats offer extended opportunities to practice.

Sharon Salzberg's *Lovingkindness: The Revolutionary Art of Happiness* explores this practice in depth and contains two dozen meditation exercises to promote lovingkindness. Salzberg writes,

> The Pali word *metta* has two root meanings. One is the word for 'gentle'.... The other root meaning for *metta* is 'friend'.... The practice of *metta*, uncovering the force of love that can uproot fear, anger and guilt, begins with befriending ourselves. The foundation of *metta* practice is to know how to be our own best friend.

Another important spiritual practice is *dana*, a Sanskrit and Pali term that denotes "gift" or "donation." *Dana* is the basis of exchange for Theravada Buddhist monks. They don't get, keep, or handle money, and instead are given, in a literal or symbolic way, what they need. Monks in turn offer their teachings for free. At Buddhadharma, retreats and instruction are free. Retreat leaders at Spirit Rock receive *dana* for their work.

Dana is not merely an economic exchange principle, however. It also represents a spiritual expression, and is, like meditation, something to be learned. In *A Path with Heart*, Kornfield writes, "Compassionate generosity is the foundation of spiritual life because it is the practice of letting go.... But for most of us, generosity is a quality that must be developed."

Steps for Beginners

Consider the possibilities. Insight meditation can be taught in a variety of ways and settings. Not all areas have *vipassana* groups that teach and practice the American-style insight meditation popularized by the Insight Meditation Society, Spirit Rock Meditation Center, and other similar centers or sitting groups. Yet teaching is readily accessible through audiotapes and videotapes. Many centers offer resources featuring their own teachers, and the best-known teachers have produced widely available tapes as well as books.

Theravada Buddhist temples that serve Southeast Asian immigrants' cultural and religious needs may also offer insight meditation instruction. Many experts on the development of Buddhism in America have commented on the distinction between "convert" Buddhism, embraced and practiced primarily by Euro-Americans born into either Judaism or Christianity, and "culture" Buddhism, practiced by those—usually Asian immigrants—born into the religion and tradition. Some temples, such as Buddhadharma, serve both groups of Buddhists. In *Old Wisdom in the New World: Americanization in Two Immigrant Theravada Buddhist Temples* (University of Tennessee Press, 1996), Buddhist scholar Paul Numrich calls this phenomenon "parallel congregations."

Such institutions offer meditation beginners a special richness in instruction, infusing cultural, religious, and practical content, all at the same time. They also offer a challenge: language differences that can affect learning and interaction. In any case, these centers are as much a part of the new Buddhism in America as are the many American-born adapters of aspects of the complex Asian Buddhist body of teachings and practices.

- Look for a good teacher. Regardless of the setting for teaching, a good teacher is crucial for a beginning meditator. Teachers and students in all traditions note that meditation can be difficult for Americans because it is so contrary to the cultural emphasis on action. A teacher is the best source of guidance when the experience of meditation prompts questions in the practitioner.

- Practice. Practice. Then practice some more.

Selected Resources

Books

Flickstein, Matthew. *Journey to the Center: A Meditation Workbook.* Boston: Wisdom Publications, 1998.

Goldstein, Joseph. *The Experience of Insight: A Simple and Direct Guide to Buddhist Meditation.* Boston: Shambhala, 1987.

———. *Insight Meditation: The Practice of Freedom.* Boston: Shambhala, 1994.

Gunaratana, Ven. Henepola. *Mindfulness in Plain English.* Boston: Wisdom Publications, 1993.

Kabat-Zinn, Jon. *Wherever You Go, There You Are: Mindfulness Meditation in Everyday Life.* New York: Hyperion, 1994.

Khema, Ayya. *When the Iron Eagle Flies: Buddhism for the West.* Boston: Wisdom Publications, 2000.

Kornfield, Jack. *A Path with Heart: A Guide through the Perils and Promises of Spiritual Life.* New York: Bantam Doubleday Dell, 1993.

Rosenberg, Larry. *Breath by Breath: The Liberating Practice of Insight Meditation.* Boston: Shambhala, 1999.

Salzberg, Sharon. *Lovingkindness: The Revolutionary Art of Happiness.* Boston: Shambhala, 1995.

Centers and organizations

Bhavana Society
Route 1, Box 218-3
High View, WV 26808
304-856-3241
www.bhavanasociety.org

Buddhadharma Buddhist Meditation Center
8910 South Kingery Highway
Hinsdale, IL 60521
630-789-8866
www.buddhistbmc.org

Insight Meditation Society
1230 Pleasant Street
Barre, MA 01005
978-355-4378
www.dharma.org

Mid America Dharma Group
P.O. Box 414411
Kansas City, MO 64141-4411
573-817-9942
www.geocities.com/Athens/3712/index

Spirit Rock Meditation Center
P.O. Box 169
Woodacre, CA 94973
415-488-0164
www.spiritrock.org

Vipassana Meditation Center/Dhamma Dara
P.O. Box 24
Shelburne, MA 01370-0024
413-625-2160
www.dhara.dhamma.org

Internet sites

- www.bcmw.org—Buddhist Council of the Midwest.

- www.dhamma.org—The international home page of organizations that offer courses in *vipassana* meditation in the tradition of teachers Sayagyi U Ba Khin and S. N. Goenka.

- www.vipassana.com—An online meditation course.

Other sources of information

Dharma Seed Tape Library
Box 66
Wendell Depot, MA 01380
800-969-7333
www.dharmaseed.org
(Offers books, audiotapes, and videotapes about Theravada *vipassana* teachings.)

Inquiring Mind
P.O. Box 9999
Berkeley, CA 94709
http://homepage.swissonline.ch/inquiringmind
(A nonprofit organization that publishes a free journal, *Inquiring Mind*, by and for the *vipassana* community.)

4

Tibetan Buddhist Meditation: Diamond Clarity

Through the methods of tantric meditation, one's usual,
habitual, ego-centered patterns of body, speech, and
mind are temporarily replaced by patterns of non-ego or
enlightened body, speech, and mind of a Buddha....
This provides gaps in the ego's shell, and the buddha-
nature can begin to shine through.

REGINALD RAY, *INDESTRUCTIBLE TRUTH:*
THE LIVING SPIRITUALITY OF TIBETAN BUDDHISM

Looking beyond Appearances

Lake Michigan, one of the five Great Lakes, is visible behind the
Shambhala Meditation Center of Chicago. On this particular day the
lake meets the horizon seamlessly, making one huge sheet of gray and
featureless cloth. Earth, water, and sky seem all of a piece, forming one
wall of the visible universe. This is a fitting backdrop for meditation, a
practice intended to penetrate this, and all, appearance.

The meditation center is located on Chicago's far north side on a
street that wraps along the lakefront like a ribbon on a gift. Squatting
on a street corner just a short walk from the lakeshore, the center

occupies a squarish, big yellow-brick house surrounded by a fence. A small sign in the front yard assures the visitor that this house is now a spiritual and public establishment rather than the private residence it once was. This has been the home of the center since 1995, when it came of age and achieved the financial sufficiency to buy the property, after functioning in a variety of rented spaces for the first twenty-five years of its life in the Chicago area.

Within, the center offers telling and distinctive detail. Compared with the visual and conceptual spareness of Zen Buddhism, the Tibetan aesthetic and sensibility come across as a busy carnival of color and detail. Like Western medieval Christianity, pictures are important within this religious tradition. Tibetan schools of spiritual practice teach visualization, the use of the mental eye, to advanced practitioners. While most religious monastics tend toward dark or drab colors, Tibetan monastics wear burgundy and gold, the former representing compassion and the latter wisdom, two cardinal Buddhist virtues. "If the tone of Zen and *vipassana* can be said to be cool, then *Vajrayana* [Tibetan] is hot," writes James W. Coleman in *The New Buddhism: The Western Transformation of an Ancient Tradition* (Oxford University Press, 2000). *Vajrayana* means "diamond vehicle," and many American practitioners of Tibetan Buddhism, especially those affiliated with Shambhala, use this term when talking about their practice. A diamond can cut through anything, and is itself indestructible; hence, *vajrayana* fittingly designates a practice of cutting through dualistic thinking. (Tibetan Buddhism is also sometimes called Tantric Buddhism, from its use of tantra, texts of special teachings attributed to the Buddha that have given rise to esoteric practices to achieve enlightenment.)

On the walls of the center, banners and *thangka*s—traditional scrolled Tibetan paintings—depict majestic beasts, part of the symbolic vocabulary of Tibetan Buddhism. One *thangka* illustrates the life of the Buddha. A large banner shows the Shambhala symbol designed by founder Chogyam Trungpa. The body of a *garuda*, a mythical winged bird, is almost covered by a shield with four symbolic representations of what are called "dignities"—important personal characteristics. A tiger represents meekness; a snow lion, perkiness or unconditional cheerfulness; the *garuda*, outrageousness or fearlessness; and the dragon, inscrutability. Elsewhere on the wall, Tibetan script, elegant and calligraphic, is framed.

Tibetan sacred art relies heavily on symbolism, intricate pattern, and an eye-boggling variety of tiny detail, exemplified in the frequently seen mandala, a circular art form symbolizing underlying order within

The shrine room at Karmê Chöling, the first U.S. meditation center founded by Chogyam Trungpa, in 1970. Thick cushions (gomden) *resting on top of larger, flat cushions* (zabuton) *provide seats for meditators. Various* thangkas, *sacred symbols, and photographs of important leaders adorn the shrine. (Photo: courtesy of Shambhala Meditation Center of Chicago)*

diverse cosmic forces. Tibetan Buddhism has a sizeable assemblage of holy figures who have also been abundantly represented in art. Artistic and ritual symbolism uses appearance to teach practitioners to look beyond appearance.

Tranquil Insight

Every Sunday morning, Shambhala Meditation Center of Chicago holds an open session of Buddhist meditation that lasts three hours. You come when you wish and sit as long as you wish. The sitting begins and ends with chanting in English, and sitting meditation is punctuated by brief walking meditation every half hour. The meditation is done in a shrine room, a visual feast of a space that contains two shrines, altarlike tables with assemblages of symbolic objects.

Meditators sit in the Tibetan Buddhist style, holding a dignified but relaxed posture, with their legs crossed and their hands resting flat, palms down, on their thighs; their eyes are to remain open but the gaze dropped. (Photo: courtesy of Karmê Chöling Shambhala Buddhist Meditation Center)

Free, individual instruction is offered in the basics of sitting meditation, called *shamatha vipashyana* (tranquil insight). Nancy, a middle-aged woman with whitish-blond hair, taps me on the shoulder in the room where we are meditating when it's my turn for instruction, and we go upstairs to one of several small rooms on the top floor. I'm used to sitting for meditation another way, so I have to learn the posture here as well as remember not to mix up sitting styles, which differ slightly across the Eastern meditation traditions.

Shamatha vipashyana is a preliminary step along the path of Buddhism as taught here. It is a way to start that involves posture, breathing, and mind. A student sits on a rectangular cushion called a *gomden*, which is positioned atop a larger, flat cushion *(zabuton)*. The *gomden* sits one up taller than the round cushion *(zafu)* customarily used in other forms of Buddhist meditation. The spine is held relaxed but straight. It helps to imagine the spine as a string being pulled up straight. Legs are crossed and hands rest flat, palms down, on the thighs. Eyes remain open but the gaze is dropped; the head remains erect. The posture is intended to be dignified but relaxed, planted firmly atop the cushion and anchored by the bones in the backside.

Next, Nancy directs my attention to my breathing. I don't have to do anything special, just notice my breath as it goes in, comes out, continuing, in, out. As thoughts arise in my mind—and they quickly do—she tells me to notice the thought, say "thinking," and then let it go, without following it, chasing it off fiercely, or starting any mental arguments. Just drop it gently and breathe, breathe, breathe.

That's it for the beginning, anyway. If I suddenly develop an itch or my leg falls asleep, Nancy tells me to try to notice it rather than immediately respond to provide relief. Meditators may also use a "resting position"—sitting with legs drawn up—if they experience pain and need to shift out of the cross-legged posture. This meditation practice is ultimately about being gentle with oneself, not sadistic or aggressive. Very often in our pragmatic American culture, we try to aggressively muscle ourselves to attainment, Nancy says. Ordering ourselves to spiritual gain can be ironically counterproductive. "'I'm going to meditate an hour a day' expresses subtle aggression," says Nancy, who is a psychologist. "Though we may think we're doing good, our attitude defeats us."

Walking meditation is also undertaken in a dignified way. Nancy gives me instructions for holding my hands correctly. The thumb of the left hand is turned down at a ninety-degree angle, the other four fingers closing around it. The right hand covers the left, and both hands are held slightly below the navel, an important center of energy in the Tibetan Buddhist understanding of the body. The foot comes down slowly and deliberately, heel, sole, toe, rippling the walker forward. The walking meditator pays attention to the action of walking in the same kind of way the sitting meditator pays attention to breathing. Walking meditation is also a physical change of pace from the seated posture, a wake-up for sleepy or stiff limbs.

The Secular Path

The converted house is filled with rooms that offer assembly spaces, classrooms, and small meeting rooms. This week the regular shrine room holds a group of advanced students gathered for a weekend of study and practice. In another room, a different group is assembled for an introductory class in Shambhala training, generally described as a secular path of spiritual training rooted in Buddhism.

This secular path is one of the distinctive features of Shambhala, which has more than one hundred locations worldwide. Center founder Trungpa, a gifted teacher who escaped Tibet in 1959 (after the Chinese invasion) and came to the United States from England in 1970, developed it as a counterpart to Buddhist religious study and practice that would apply elements of Buddhism within a secular setting and appeal to those without interest in religion. This training, Buddhist meditation and study, and other classes and activities constitute a number of accessible entry points into the Tibetan tradition that has been transplanted out of that historic mountain kingdom into exile and into the West. Shambhala operates five residential centers for intensive religious study and practice: two in Canada, two in the United States, and one in France. Its principal teacher is Sakyong Mipham Rinpoche, son and spiritual heir of Trungpa, who died in 1987.

Instructors work with beginning meditators by asking them periodically about their experiences while sitting. Beginners have questions, are sometimes overzealous, and sometimes unintentionally sloppy. "We correct tightness and looseness," says Nancy. She and others at the center like to recommend the more systematic training in meditation that forms the initial part of the Shambhala training that is generally thought of as the secular path. The first several weeks of training introduce the tool of meditation.

Meditation classes distinct from the Shambhala training are also offered. Special workshops with visiting teachers from within the Shambhala organization are regularly scheduled. Each individual center thereby has access to a larger core of resources. Other contemplative practices are periodically taught. One new offering at the center is *kyudo*, the way of the bow. In this contemplative archery practice, the focus is on "polishing the mind" rather than developing marksmanship. The center has a bookstore with a variety of titles and periodicals, as well as other items useful to a student's spiritual practice.

The Shrine Room: A Stronghold of Color and Symbolism

Filled with visual and symbolic references to teachers, beliefs, and practices, the shrine room, where meditation customarily takes place, is a schoolroom in itself that teaches a lot about Tibetan Buddhism and Shambhala. In keeping with Shambhala's development of two paths of practice, there are two shrines: one explicitly Buddhist and one called the Shambhala shrine.

The warrior's shrine

The Shambhala warrior's shrine—someone following the secular Shambhala path of meditation and study is thought of as a "warrior" because the path requires courage—includes an array of simple, highly symbolic objects. Five clear offering bowls are filled with objects, each object related to a different physical sense—sight, sound, smell, taste, touch. Behind the row of offering bowls are three jars: one filled with ink, signifying the warrior's tender blood and loyalty to the lineage of warriors; one filled with tea, signifying the energy of cutting through conceptual mind and discursive thought; and one filled with sake, signifying the intoxicating and emotional quality of the Great Eastern Sun, a vision of human power and dignity. Candles signify the warrior's discipline of constant awareness, so they are lit when the shrine room is in use.

A large ink brush is the weapon of the warrior, who is characterized by fearlessness, gentleness, and discriminating awareness. It sits atop a piece of paper. Behind the brush is a banner with a single bold *ashe,* or calligraphic stroke, signifying the warrior's confident heart. An arrow, another warrior object, is tied with a white scarf, a symbolic overlay marking "victory over war." Two vases of flowers are symmetrically placed on either side of the Shambhala shrine.

The Buddhist shrine

The Buddhist shrine has some comparable items. Clear offering bowls—there are five, but there may be as few as three or as many as seven—hold water, offerings of generosity to the lineage of enlightened beings.

Positioned on a round plate—a mandala plate—are five offerings of rice, related to the five components of the self (*skandhas*—form, sensation, perception, mental formations, and consciousness). On top of the rice is a scepter, intended to represent the *vajra*, expressing skillful means and the indestructible quality of enlightenment. Its placement signifies the transformation of the *skandhas* into five Buddha wisdoms. Three small statues (*rupas*, meaning "forms") represent Manjushri, the bodhisattva (enlightened being) of wisdom; the Buddha in meditative posture; and Milarepa, a historic and significant teacher in Tibetan Buddhism.

A crystal sphere symbolizes the clarity of enlightened mind. Two different urns hold relics; one of them contains a piece of bone from Shambhala founder Trungpa. (After Trungpa's death in 1987, most of the Shambhala centers established then were given some cremated remains.) Wrapped in brocade and occupying a place of honor in the shrine is a text, signifying dharma (teachings of the Buddha and other enlightened teachers).

Four photos above the shrine depict important leaders for Shambhala. The sixteenth Gyalwa Karmapa headed the Karma lineage of the Kagyu school within Tibetan Buddhism, of which Shambhala considers itself a part. The Kagyu school is one of four major schools, or transmissions, of Tibetan Buddhism, each stemming from and including different significant teachers. Another photo shows Dilgo Khyentse Rinpoche, a prominent teacher in the Nyingma school, considered Tibetan Buddhism's oldest school. Although Trungpa trained in the Kagyu school, he also was in the Nyingma lineage through his "root guru," or principal teacher. Shambhala founder Trungpa is depicted, as is current Shambhala leader Sakyong Mipham Rinpoche, Trungpa's successor as spiritual head of Shambhala and also his son.

As with the other Buddhist traditions, lineage—the succession of teachers—is important. Buddhism considers itself a living tradition, passed along through direct teaching over time and generations. A lineage tries to trace its links back to the Buddha, although significant historic teachers have carved out many branches off the stream of the historic Buddha's teaching.

Tibetan Buddhism also embraces the practice of guru devotion. A teacher represents, in a deep way, the Buddha himself. Tibetan Buddhism includes guru yoga—practices that accord the teacher an esteemed position and that express a form of devotion intended not to sanctify the teacher but to help the student attain enlightenment.

Between the two main shrines, a chair is placed, signifying the continual presence of the guru—in this case, both Trungpa and his son. Next to the chair is a small table with a candle and a gold Japanese hand fan—both items used by Trungpa and Mipham Rinpoche during teaching—and flowers.

A shrine to Black Mahakala

A third shrine is less prominent in Shambhala-Chicago's shrine room. It is a shrine to Black Mahakala, a deity considered to be a protector of the teachings *(dharmapala)*. A *thangka*—painted scroll—displays a wrathful, black-skinned figure, mouth full of fanged teeth. Mahakala is understood as time, the devourer of everything, hence the teeth. Arranged in front of the Black Mahakala are a candle, to signify the protector's presence, and an offering cup filled with black tea.

Complexity and depth

The shrine room is festooned with colorful brocaded banners, adorned with various auspicious signs from the vocabulary of Tibetan symbolism. Other deities or enlightened beings are depicted on still more scrolls. This highly detailed visual display hints at the entire complexity and richness of the panoply of spiritual practices and teachings in Tibetan Buddhism, a branch or way of Buddhism that engages the human faculties of mind and sense and physical energy in a distinctive spiritual jet propulsion toward enlightenment. "Tibetan Buddhism contains more practices, more meditation techniques, and studies more different schools of Buddhist philosophy than any of the other Buddhist traditions," writes Coleman in *The New Buddhism*.

Chogyam Trungpa had his critics, who raised questions about the flamboyant way he chose to live out his teachings. He deliberately used outrageousness—what he called "crazy wisdom"—in his teaching, and would often lecture in a three-piece suit, waving a paper hand fan and sipping a glass of sake. Yet few would argue that he was one of the most influential interpreters and planters of Tibetan Buddhism in the West. Trungpa skillfully translated the teachings of his tradition into Western psychological terms, into terms that apply in everyday life.

Practitioners' Stories

Peter: "Start with disappointment"

Peter McLaughlin, director of the center, notes that Trungpa counsels, in his seminal work *Cutting through Spiritual Materialism*, that Buddhism is about learning to deal with disappointment.

> We must surrender our hopes and expectations, as well
> as our fears, and march directly into disappointment,
> work with disappointment, go into it and make it our
> way of life.... Disappointment is the best chariot to use
> on the path to the *dharma*.

"Disappointment is inherent in the human condition," McLaughlin says, "but there are ways to find joy within the process of living."

McLaughlin, fifty, has been a practitioner within the Shambhala school since the early 1970s. He remembers reading a newspaper story about Trungpa when the latter first came to Chicago; it described the

Tibetan teacher, McLaughlin recalls, as "the least likely entrant in the great guru sweepstakes." "He was dressed in a three-piece suit, he was smoking a cigarette and drinking what turned out to be a glass of sake." This, and the fact that the story mentioned the frequent laughter that punctuated the interview, intrigued the then twenty-three-year-old, who had already been reading about meditation. One book he had encountered was the influential *The Three Pillars of Zen*, which started him meditating.

"But the notion of going off to a Zen center and shaving my head and wearing black robes and sitting in that style didn't appeal to my twenty-three-year-old nature," McLaughlin explains. "I had read a thing or two prior to that, along with a great deal of many other teachings, and suddenly it all kind of crystallized."

The teachings of Trungpa, with their immediate relevance, and his distinctive style, which spoke persuasively to thousands of Americans seeking a meditative spiritual path, did appeal to McLaughlin, who continued to practice and study at the center—known as the Dharmadhatu Center until 1995—as it moved several times through the 1970s and early 1980s. His path was gradual and slow, part of what made it take deep root in his life. This is in keeping with the Shambhala school, McLaughlin says. "Trungpa Rinpoche wanted us to meditate for a very, very long time, and to study also, so we weren't dumb meditators," he says. "For me, this gradual approach, this 'non-trippy' approach, worked. [Trungpa] didn't want people thinking this was something other than regular life."

McLaughlin has an eminently regular and secular life that keeps paychecks coming into his household. He is a stationary engineer, operating the heating, ventilating, and air-conditioning systems in a high-rise office building. He is also the father of an adult son who took part at the age of eight in a rite-of-passage ceremony, a special ceremony in the Shambhala community that marks a child's maturation.

"There's an interesting element of discovery in all of this. It is a process of discovery, like poetry," says McLaughlin, who majored in English while in college and met fabled beat poet Allen Ginsberg during some advanced Shambhala training. "I'm not going after some kind of reward at the end of my lifetime. It is actually rewarding now."

John: "Meditation fits with everything"

John is another longtime student at the Shambhala Center. He attended a weekend meditation program with Chogyam Trungpa when the teacher visited Chicago in the early 1970s. John was already reading about meditation. "In those days there was quite a bit available," says John, who is now forty-eight and was then a college student.

"Meditation fits with everything," he says. "It's a way of checking in with your mind."

John has a six-foot-five-inch, lean frame neatly dressed in good chinos and a sport coat, Sunday-church quality clothes he wears regularly to the center, since Trungpa, who liked to upend people's expectations by wearing suits instead of exotic Tibetan garb, encouraged his students to give some thought to their appearance. "It's part of our tradition," John says about his appearance.

He stops to think about what captured his attention about Trungpa's teachings and encouraged him to keep coming back. "It felt real," he says with his slow, deliberate voice. "It felt like it touched my life. I could blend the practice with my life and vice versa." Today, he works as a paramedic for the Chicago fire department. While his occupation might strike some as stressful, the flash points in his life come from personal relationships. "That's where the sharp edges come," he says.

He is deeply involved in the local Shambhala community, frequently attending functions and taking part in the council that handles the business of the center. "It's kind of like I live here," he says.

When John was a child, he was raised in a Christian tradition that didn't make much of an impression on him. "I bounced around," he says, "and religion was something imposed from outside." Instead, he considers himself to have "grown up Buddhist," in a deeper, formative sense.

"I just feel like it's the right thing to do," he says of his years of practice and study. "It's how I choose to live my life."

Ella: "You learn to tame your mind"

The teachings Trungpa adapted for those outside his native mountain kingdom spoke to others besides Americans. Ella, another Shambhala student, first encountered Buddhism in her native Ukraine. "I always thought there was something more," she says, explaining how her spiritual curiosity drove her to Eastern traditions. First she was attracted to the Hindu tradition; she and other friends became vegetarians, wore white clothes, and listened to Indian music. Although she could read books translated into Russian, meditation teachers were not to be found in the Ukraine, nor, theoretically, could anything at all remotely religious be located or practiced. It was the 1980s, a time when communism, which disavows religion and officially bars religious practice, was in power, and Ukraine was part of the Soviet Union. "We had problems with the KGB [secret police]," says Ella. The KGB confiscated her books—the translations were deemed illegal—and notes.

"I was more brave then," says Ella, who is now a very youthful looking forty-one, with a dismissive laugh.

Ultimately, however, Ella's interests led her to Buddhism. She explains how Buddhism helps her understand the workings of her own mind and its crannies: what practitioners like the Dalai Lama would call "mental afflictions" but Trungpa would refer to as "neuroses."

"It's about completely being in the present moment," she says. "You just face it. You learn to see your mind; you learn about your mind and to tame your mind."

Ella's ability to practice increased in the late 1980s, when *perestroika* and Mikhail Gorbachev brought openness to Eastern Europe. Her parents immigrated in 1987 to the Chicago area, and she began visiting them regularly. During one of her visits to her family, she decided also to visit a meditation center, and so began calling around. People at Shambhala-Chicago, then known as Dharmadhatu, called her back. She went to meditate there and knew immediately, and deeply, she was in the right place, an experience common to others as they come into a Buddhist center for the first time. "I had immediately this feeling that I came home," she says. "Even people's faces were kind of familiar to me."

So each time Ella returned to visit her parents, she also returned to the Shambhala center. The pull of possibilities grew so strong that she finally decided to move to this country three years ago. She is now studying psychology at a local community college and working in a public library.

Ella thinks of her move to the United States as "starting over," and her spiritual practice and studies are an important part of her life here. Last summer she went to what is called "seminary" in the Shambhala school: a three-month period of intensive study and practice at a retreat center. Students who attend seminary then move on to further studies, which they usually call *vajrayana* practice. This can include many elements, among them prostrations, an expression of taking refuge in the Buddha; a variety of meditation techniques and visualizations; and symbolic purification practices. But *shamatha vipashyana*—basic meditation—remains a fundamental practice for all students.

Attending seminary was an especially meaningful step along the path for Ella. "This is a step when you begin to belong to the lineage of Buddha," she says. "I feel very honored."

Ella lives with her parents, who were born Jewish but did not practice their faith in the Ukraine. At first, she says, they were skeptical about her involvement with Tibetan Buddhism. But she began inviting friends from the center over, and they were able to allay her parents' doubts. "My parents are now curious," she says. She hopes to apply what she is learning through meditation into a career in this country in social work. "I want to work with people and use my meditation and experience to help people. When you see what's going on, half the work is done."

Charles: "Certain mysteries come up for contemplation"

Charles, another Shambhala student, says that he was maybe eleven or twelve years old when he began investigating religious possibilities other than the Roman Catholicism in which he was raised. "My dad was interested in talking about different things, and that drove me to the library," Charles says. "I began reading anything I could get my hands on in different traditions."

By the time he attended Beloit College in Wisconsin in 1967, he was ready to study anthropology and comparative religions, and to sample life in a Hindu Vedanta monastery. He spent four months in one in Chicago in 1968, then returned in the early 1970s. "I wanted to check out whether I wanted to live a monastic life," he says.

He found out he didn't, and so went instead to the East Coast, where he pursued a variety of interests and studies, none of them definitive. Among his interests was Buddhism. He remembers meeting Trungpa at an arts festival in Boston in 1974; he also remembers hearing Allen Ginsberg, a follower of Trungpa's, recite poetry at the same festival at which Trungpa spoke. But Charles, who had extricated himself from a monastery, was a little leery about "teacher-hopping." He worked in a factory and studied art history until he decided to move to Chicago, where he prepared to become a chiropractor. On his graduation from chiropractic school in 1981, something was pulling at his sleeve. He had big pieces of his life—a career, a marriage—in place, but something was missing.

"I literally felt I needed to sit down and think about things, and I had meditated in past," he recalls. By the early 1980s, Buddhism was a bit less of an exotic and nascent practice in this country. "I had been saying, 'I'm basically Buddhist,' but I wasn't really practicing, so I thought, 'Well, okay, I'll check out various meditation centers.'"

He was already on the mailing list for the Dharmadhatu (Shambhala) center, and he remembers that one day he got a mailing from them about an upcoming weekend training, and they also called the same day to invite him. Although he was apprehensive about spending more than an hour in meditation, he signed on.

"I made it through the first weekend and I was like, 'This is okay, I like this.' I'd been doing a lot of reading on my own in Tibetan Buddhism and I decided that the values appealed to me." Slowly, as he took classes and became more deeply involved, more pieces began to come together.

"Buddhism has been a major interest in my life since I was twelve," says Charles, who is now fifty-two. "As I began to practice, some of the things I read about began to make sense. That was what I liked about Trungpa: he made things pretty day-to-day ordinary. You'd read these things in books and they sounded trippy and bizarre, but they're just talking about the experience of life. I could work with this and begin to study and learn."

Although he doesn't want to stretch the comparison, Charles says that his spiritual practice today, almost twenty years later, is a little bit like the discipline followed by Catholic priests and nuns who pray the Divine Hours, a set of prayers said daily to punctuate and give meaning to everyday activities.

"*Vajrayana* practice is very much specifically a regimen to continue to work with certain values and insights on a regular basis," he says. "Certain mysteries, certain teachings come up for your contemplation... like in the Catholic tradition, where the priests and brothers and nuns say the Divine Hours. It's not identical, but that's what it's like."

Variety Meets Complexity: Other Approaches, Other Teachers

Other approaches

Shambhala offers Westerners one accessible approach to Tibetan Buddhism. Bristling with symbolism and mystery, Tibetan Buddhism can be difficult for beginners to navigate. It has four major schools, developed over time and associated with key teachers who interpreted the basic teachings and practices of the Buddha. It also contains a variety of religious practices and disciplines, and its cosmology and symbolism are elaborately detailed. While Tibetan Buddhism embraces many practices in addition to meditation, meditation has been adapted by gifted and exiled Tibetan teachers in the West as a basic practice. The practice can also be a gate into the vast world of Tibetan teachings, figures, cosmology, and history, which is unique to the culture while also having been shaped by the Buddhist religion that Tibet shares with its Asian neighbors.

The designation *vajrayana* (diamond vehicle) recognizes the uniqueness of the Tibetan variant of Buddhism. The Sanskrit term *yana* means "vehicle," a conveyance that one chooses for one's spiritual journey. Mahayana Buddhism—*mahayana* means "great vehicle" and is concerned with saving all sentient beings—is the umbrella term for variants practiced in China, India, Korea, and Japan, including Zen. Tibetan Buddhism is also Mahayanist, but it is often viewed as a separate vehicle. Theravada Buddhism, practiced in Southeast Asian countries, is the third major Buddhist tradition; it regards itself as closest to the "original" Buddhism taught by the Buddha himself. This triad of Buddhisms is sometimes referred to as the three wheels *(dharmachakra)*.

More so than the other traditions of Buddhism, Tibetan Buddhism has esoteric teachings and practices that are not taught to beginners and are considered secret. These teachings are to be passed on orally, from teacher to student. Buddhism is preeminently a religion of both study and practice, and the Buddhism that developed in Tibet offers many practices, including visualizations, prostrations, devotions, chanting, and practices that explore expressions of human energies. Tibetan Buddhism places emphasis on tantra. *Tantra* means "thread," but it also connotes interpenetration, much as threads are woven together by a weaver. The hidden nature of tantra teaching and practice is a defining feature of Tibetan Buddhism, becoming revealed to those who choose to explore and practice in depth.

Paradoxically enough, given its complexity of practices, Tibetan Buddhism is often considered the "quick path" within Buddhism, understood within the context of reincarnation. Tibetan Buddhism holds that enlightenment—the pure awareness of the nature of existence that is

Members of Shambhala Meditation Center of Chicago gather on Shambhala Day, a celebration of the Tibetan New Year. They are listening to a dharma talk; listening to teaching is one way of developing a meditation practice. In Tibetan Buddhism, teachers are highly esteemed authorities. (Photo: courtesy of Shambhala Meditation Center of Chicago)

the goal of Buddhism—can be gained within a single lifetime through skillful practice.

Other teachers

Its practices are complex, its teachers multiple. Coleman writes in *The New Buddhism*, "There is a saying in Tibet that 'every valley has a different *lama* (teacher),' and each of those lamas has their own way of teaching." As is the case in Zen Buddhism and insight meditation, different teachers and their lineages may have different styles or emphases. A beginner's experience of meditation may accordingly differ by source.

As Trungpa taught Tibetan Buddhism, *shamatha vipashyana* can be considered a fundamental practice; some other Tibetan Buddhists teach a kind of "formless" meditation to more advanced students. Lama Surya Das, an American who studied with Tibetan teachers in India and France, teaches *dzogchen*. *Dzogchen*, which means "great perfection," is regarded in traditional Tibetan teaching as an advanced meditation practice. But in books such as *Awakening the Buddha Within: Tibetan Wisdom for the Western World*, Surya Das has tried to make advanced teachings and techniques accessible to Westerners less extensively schooled in Tibetan Buddhism.

The Dalai Lama is certainly the world's best-known practitioner, and symbol, of Tibetan Buddhism. Popular works by him, such as *The Art of Happiness* (Riverhead, 1998), have been best-sellers, offering a simple application to contemporary life of core teachings of Buddhism. The Dalai Lama is best known in the West as the political leader of the Tibetan diaspora—Tibetans driven from their homeland by the Chinese invasion of 1959—albeit a leader with spiritual as well as political authority. His large body of written work includes transcriptions of highly accessible public talks as well as teachings based on Tibetan sacred texts.

Tarthang Tulku was one of the first Tibetan teachers to establish a base in the United States. In 1973, Tarthang founded the Nyingma Institute in Berkeley, California, a residential center for teaching, translation, training in Buddhist psychology, publishing, and long-term study.

Many of the influential Tibetan teachers who came to America were from the Kagyu school of Tibetan Buddhism, a school known for its emphasis on practice. Kagyu teacher Kalu Rinpoche was among the earliest wave of Tibetans to reach and teach Westerners. Like many teachers in the 1970s and 1980s, he traveled the country extensively, and established a major retreat center in New York, Kagyu Thubten Chöling.

Karma Triyana Dharmachakra is a New York state monastery that is also the heart of a network of meditation centers throughout North America. It represents the Tibetan teaching lineage of the Gyalwa Karmapa, another important figure.

Another network of Tibetan meditation centers throughout the United States and Canada follows the teachings of Geshe Kelsang Gyatso, who traces his lineage to the teachings of Jey Tsong Khapa, a thirteenth-century figure who made significant contributions to the Tibetan Buddhist tradition. Found in a number of cities, these centers make up the Kadampa network.

Steps for Beginners

Beginning meditators interested in Tibetan Buddhism will find a rich and elaborate tradition. By its very nature, Tibetan Buddhism contains mysteries—esoteric wisdom—and this has helped promote a popular mystique about it. While that mystique is currently fueled by celebrity interest in and sympathy for Tibetan religion and culture, it has always been part of the Western understanding of this remote mountain country, historically associated with the mythical paradise of Shangri-la. So a little reality-testing research is a good idea in approaching the prospect of meditation and spiritual practice in the Tibetan Buddhist tradition.

▨ Understand the teacher and his or her background. As with other Buddhist traditions, continuity of teaching—expressed in lineage—is a good indicator of what to expect. Who are the teacher's teachers? A multiplicity of voices enriches any interpretation.

Some of the mystery around Tibetan Buddhism can be dissipated simply by decoding the titles given to various kinds of teachers. Different titles distinguish Tibetan teachers. *Lama* is the most general term for teacher; it is also used as a polite form of address for any Tibetan monk. *Tulku* is a title designating a teacher who is a reincarnation of a deceased distinguished teacher. *Geshe* signifies a teacher with advanced and extensive academic training; the title is not common. *Rinpoche,* an honorific title, means "jewel" or "precious one," and distinguishes an especially skillful teacher.

The match between teacher and student is especially important. Tibetan Buddhist teaching emphasizes this relationship, and spiritual development takes place through it. Sometimes a student may be given visualization or meditation practices that represent the teacher as an enlightened being with whom the student seeks spiritual identification. So a teacher serves a function that is more spiritual than pedagogical.

▨ Read, a little. Books have been called a dharma (teaching) gate, and they can help provide support for individual practice. Many meditators begin by reading among world religions, which helps to broaden the universe of possibilities. Works within and about Tibetan Buddhism will continue to grow and circulate more widely as more Westerners gain scholarly and practical access to teachers and teachings and demonstrate the contemporary applications of wisdom that developed centuries and worlds apart from here and now.

▨ Be aware of other sources of information: With appropriate irony, the preservation and propagation of timeless

Tibetan teachings is also taking place through technology. A number of monasteries and centers have extensive websites that offer introductions to their traditions. (See the list of selected resources.)

Advanced Tibetan Buddhism is a rigorous mix of ritual, practice, and understanding that a beginner will only see glimpses of. Should these be the spiritual mountains that beckon, the view from them is said to be enlightening.

Selected Resources

Books

Chodron, Pema. *Start Where You Are: A Guide to Compassionate Living.* Boston: Shambhala, 1994.

Chodron, Thubten. *Buddhism for Beginners.* Ithaca, N.Y.: Snow Lion Publications, 2001.

McDonald, Kathleen. *How to Meditate: A Practical Guide.* Boston: Wisdom Publications, 1995.

Ray, Reginald. *Indestructible Truth: The Living Spirituality of Tibetan Buddhism.* Boston: Shambhala, 2000.

Rinpoche, Kalu. *Gently Whispered: Oral Teachings by the Very Venerable Kalu Rinpoche.* Barrytown, N.Y.: Station Hill Press, 1994.

Rinpoche, Sogyal. *The Tibetan Book of Living and Dying.* San Francisco: Harper San Francisco, 1992.

Surya Das, Lama. *Awakening the Buddha Within: Tibetan Wisdom for the Western World.* New York: Broadway Books, 1997.

Trungpa, Chogyam. *Cutting through Spiritual Materialism.* Boulder, Colo.: Shambhala, 1973.

———. *The Path Is the Goal: A Basic Handbook of Buddhist Meditation.* Boston: Shambhala, 1995.

Tulku, Tarthang. *Hidden Mind of Freedom.* Berkeley, Calif.: Dharma Publishing, 1981.

Yeshe, Lama, and Zopa Rinpoche, Lama. *Wisdom Energy: Basic Buddhist Teachings*. Boston: Wisdom Publications, 2000.

Centers and organizations

Foundation for the Preservation of the Mahayana Tradition
125B La Posta Road
Taos, NM 87571
505-758-7766
www.fpmt.org

Kagyu Thubten Chöling Monastery and Retreat Center
245 Sheafe Road
Wappingers Falls, New York 12590
845-297-2500
www.kagyu.com

Karma Triyana Dharmachakra
352 Meads Mountain Road
Woodstock, NY 12498
914-679-4625
www.kagyu.org

Nyingma Institute
1815 Highland Place
Berkeley, CA 94709
510-843-6812
www.nyingmainstitute.com

Rigpa U.S.
449 Powell Street, Suite 200
San Francisco, CA 94102
415-392-2055
www.rigpa.org

Shambhala International
1084 Tower Road
Halifax, Nova Scotia
B3H 2Y5 Canada
902-425-4275
www.shambhala.org

Internet sites

- www.kadampa.net—Home page for the network of New Kadampa tradition centers established by Geshe Kelsang Gyatso and headquartered in England.

Other sources of information

Shambhala Sun
1345 Spruce Street
Boulder, CO 80302-4886
902-422-8404
www.shambhalasun.com
(A magazine that brings a Buddhist contemplative perspective to all the important issues in modern life.)

Snow Lion Library of Tibetan Buddhism and Culture
P.O. Box 6483
Ithaca, NY 14851-6483
800-950-0313 or 607-273-8519
www.snowlionpub.com
(A publishing company providing books on Tibetan Buddhism and culture, free online newsletters, resource listings, and related links.)

5

Hindu Meditation: That Thou Art

*There was once a Hindu queen, who so much desired
that all her children attain freedom in this life that she
herself took all the care of them; and as she rocked them
to sleep, she always sang the one song to them—'Tat
tvam asi, tat tvam asi' ("That thou art, that thou art").*

SWAMI VIVEKANANDA, *MEDITATION AND ITS METHODS*

Many Pathways to God

Meditation at the Himalayan Institute Midwest offers a breath of
fresh air.

Marian, the teacher, works with only two of us students in this meditation class, which makes it fairly personal, like private instruction.
Appropriately for beginners, the class is held inside a preschool; the
Institute is renting space. The walls are papered with colorful drawings,
vocabulary words, numbers. The children who come here are uncon-
sciously absorbing a way of life as well as their small, explicit lessons.
My classmate and I will start to learn all of what yoga encompasses.

Meditation is one of the eight "limbs"—practices—of the kind of
yoga we are learning. Americans usually understand yoga as a system of

postures. A series of physical movements—part of a larger discipline of spiritual practices—is indeed called *hatha* yoga; this part of yoga deals with control of the body. Yoga in its literal sense, however, means "yoke"; it is the name for a system of practices to attain a spiritual goal: union— yoking—with God. Meditation is one yogic practice.

The world's most ancient living religion, Hinduism is rich in systems, philosophies, practices, and paths leading to union with God, or Brahman. (Brahman is understood as the transcendent state of God, impersonal, infinite, and indescribable.) The Hindu tradition from India rests on several thousand years of sacred texts, commentaries, and the lives and practices of men and women considered to be saints or sages who added to, applied, and reinterpreted this spiritual wisdom tradition and what it says about God and the many ways to God.

A hallmark of Hinduism is its recognition of differences among individuals, offering different paths, or yogas, which appeal to different personality types. There is *jnana* yoga, the path of knowledge or wisdom, which emphasizes discriminating the true from the false, the real from the unreal; *karma* yoga, the path of action; *bhakti* yoga, the way of love or devotion in which the seeker relates to a personalized idea of God; and *raja* yoga.

Meditation is part of the whole set of practices that make up *raja* yoga. *Raja* means "royal"; this pathway to God allows us to experience divine union through a gradual process of purification of body and concentration of mind. Undertaking the process enhances health, reduces impediments to spiritual development, and develops the transcendent capabilities of the mind. Hence, meditation within the Hindu tradition is not a stand-alone technique or path to God; it is one conveyance of many used on the spiritual journey.

Meditation instruction at the Himalayan Institute Midwest is both detailed and systematic, a mix of explanation of principles and techniques and chances to practice them. In the first in a series of seven classes, we begin by learning about the eight limbs.

1. Restraints *(yamas)*: These include non-harming, non-lying, non-stealing, non-possessiveness, and sexual and sensual restraint. These standards constitute a form of "don'ts"; they restrain impulses to harmful or excessive behaviors.

2. Observances *(niyamas)*: These are behaviors to be practiced, including cleanliness, both physical and mental; contentment; study, which embraces self-study; self-discipline; and self-surrender, understood as a surrender of ego and submission to God.

3. Postures *(asanas)*: These include the postures or poses generally thought of in the West as yoga, specific and varied ways of manipulating and exercising the body. They also refer to different sitting postures for meditation.

4. Breath control *(pranayama)*: This limb teaches exercises for control of breath, or *prana*, which is understood as energy. Breath control affects the flow of energy in the body and hence affects the mind, facilitating concentration. Breathing exercises manipulate the breath in different ways to achieve different effects. Experienced yogis always counsel caution in the practice of types of breath control, because the practice has potential to cause harm if done incorrectly. The guidance of a teacher is needed.

5. Sense withdrawal *(pratyahara)*: This step involves closing the eyes to cut off visual stimulation, but we also learn techniques for systematically relaxing the entire body to shepherd attention inward to prepare to concentrate.

6. Concentration *(dharana)*: Eastern wisdom traditions understand concentration as one-pointed or single-minded attention to an object. Concentration thus contrasts with "formless" meditation, in which awareness

expands without being focused on a particular object. Yogic concentration often uses special sacred sounds called mantras as the object of concentration.

7. Meditation *(dhyana)*: *Dhyana* is the Sanskrit word that is the origin of the Chinese term *ch'an* and the Japanese term *zen*, associated with Buddhist systems of meditation. In the Hindu tradition, concentration precedes meditation, the uninterrupted flow of the mind toward a mental object.

8. *Samadhi:* This term is sometimes used in the original Sanskrit because there is no English equivalent that fully conveys its connotations. Sometimes rendered as "absorption" or "realization" or "superconsciousness," it is a state of unity in which the mind merges with the object of meditation. Now, there is no longer any duality, no longer a distinction between subject and object. *Samadhi* is said to be a condition of ecstasy. In its highest development, it is equivalent to self-realization or enlightenment.

Swami Rama (*swami* means "master," and is the term for Hindu monks), founder of the Himalayan Institute, says this of *samadhi* in *Meditation and Its Practice:* "There are various types of samadhi, but I can tell you that a meditator is fully capable of attaining the highest state of wisdom, in which the mind cannot and does not pose any questions, because all questions are answered and all problems resolved."

With this hierarchy laid out at the beginning, it's clear that we'll be doing more than just sitting on a cushion. There is much preparation in the areas of stretching and breathing.

Marian shows us a number of simple stretching exercises that work on body and mind. We concentrate on standing still in the mountain pose, noticing the spine and keeping it erect, as if it were a string being pulled up straight. We pay attention to bending back, forward, side to side, stretching fully but gently, using muscles without straining them, almost like acknowledging them and urging them to get on board for the meditative journey.

Then we learn the corpse pose, which is a basic one. It is practiced lying down flat, face up, eyes closed, arms held slightly away from body and palms up, legs slightly apart. We breathe evenly, no jerks or pauses or holding breath, scanning areas of the body to check for tension, moving the attention slowly from area to area. The corpse pose is a way of relaxing the body and gathering the mind on the task.

Within Hinduism, meditation is not a stand-alone technique but is one of eight "limbs" that make up raja yoga, an interrelated system of practices of purification of the body and concentration of the mind that leads the practitioner to union with God. (Photo: Donnell Collins)

Breath as Vital Energy

Becoming acquainted with breath, training it, and manipulating it in different patterns are a critical part of the yogic preparation for meditation. "Our breath reflects the state of our mind at all times," writes Swami Rama in *Meditation and Its Practice.* Breathing patterns change in response to events and stimuli in our lives; shallow breathing is a common practice and a sign of chronic stress. Breath is not merely some incidental and mechanical element in our makeup; it is energy to be tapped and harnessed as an expression of spirit, as part of spiritual development. Wisdom texts in this tradition lay out a whole science of breath. We learn a few basics of breath consciousness.

Diaphragmatic breathing is essential to physical and spiritual health. Marian gives us exercises to increase our awareness of the role of the diaphragm, one of the body's largest muscles. She also shows us how to check which nostril is the more active in breathing. In yoga, the breath is understood as naturally alternating and cyclic, one nostril dominant, the other passive, reflecting cycles of subtle energy. We learn different patterns of alternate nostril breathing, done to balance energy flow.

Marian also teaches us a few different postures for sitting. To my surprise, one of them, the friendship pose, actually uses a chair, so that the beginning meditator can start without physical discomfort. For those who are more flexible and able to sit on the floor, the easy pose is just that—easy. Legs are crossed and knees rest on feet. In a more advanced seated posture, the legs are crossed differently and the knees are brought to the floor, giving a wider and more stable base.

In the Institute's teaching of meditation, the classic full-lotus pose is not used for meditation; it's too uncomfortable for most Westerners. Emphasis is less on what the legs do and more on trunk alignment to facilitate diaphragmatic breathing. Underlying these practices is an elaborate science of yoga, covering psychology and physiology. All this stretching and breathing are an essential part of the mind-body approach to yoga meditation.

The Himalayan Institute Midwest is headquartered in the larger northern suburb of Evanston, but it also offers classes at two satellite locations; this preschool in the western Chicago suburb of Prospect Heights is one of them. Satellite centers make yoga practice more accessible to students like Rashna, who lives nearby. She enrolled in the meditation class at the recommendation of her husband, who had taken a hatha yoga class and was enthusiastic about its results. Rashna, a physical therapist, was hesitant about her ability to do and benefit from hatha yoga because of neck and back problems. Now she plans to take another meditation class and then go on to hatha yoga.

Although she has a six-year-old child and a job, she tries to make time to meditate each day and practice what she is learning. "I say, 'Oh, I have the time today,' and then, absolutely, I do it." Rashna brings her questions to class each week to check things with Marian: "Am I doing this right?" "Why is my mind so busy and unable to concentrate?"

Though Rashna was born in India, she is not a Hindu but a Parsi, an adherent of the ancient Persian faith known as Zoroastrianism. Little of what she is learning is familiar, though she recognizes some of the Sanskrit terms. But the content is quite compatible with her own religion, which emphasizes ethical values. "It does fit in very well," she says.

Rashna is interested in meditation primarily as a technique for relaxing rather than as a tool for spiritual development. "When I'm doing meditation, I'm not thinking of anything spiritual *or* material," she says. "I focus on one little point so that I can go blank on all other things."

The Bigger Picture: What Practitioners Say

The Himalayan Institute Midwest encourages a holistic view of spirituality. It is part of an international network of centers affiliated with the Himalayan International Institute of Yoga Science and Philosophy in Honesdale, Pennsylvania. Founded in 1971 by Swami Rama, the institute incorporates Western principles of health and psychology into its teaching and training in yoga, psychology and self-development, and meditation and holistic health. The Himalayan Institute operates a Center for Health and Healing; it also offers training and certification for teachers of yoga. It maintains a residency program for interested students.

Founder Swami Rama studied yoga and meditation in his native India, attended Oxford University in England, and trained under a spiritual master in Tibet. In 1969 he came to the United States as a research consultant to the Menninger Foundation on a project studying voluntary control of internal states. Swami Rama was able to demonstrate in laboratory settings his voluntary control of autonomic functioning such as heart rate and breath—a power he had attained through yoga. Subsequently he traveled and lectured in the United States. He also founded the Himalayan Institute Hospital and Medical City in his native region in the Himalayan foothills of northern India, 125 miles north of New Delhi. Swami Rama died in 1996.

Jerome: "Yoga is the whole path"

Himalayan Institute Midwest director Jerome Smith spent two years working at the hospital complex in India. He worked in the physical therapy department, teaching yoga postures and breathing techniques. "The overall experience of living in another culture was very growthful," he says, "and it changed me in definite yet subtle ways."

Smith, who is forty, first became aware of Eastern wisdom through the television show *Kung Fu*, which was popular in his childhood. "I liked the Eastern sages, I liked that outlook on life, the non-harming," he says. As he grew, his interest did also, and he read about yoga and the Hindu tradition. He also was curious about and intrigued by the prospect of living in a monastery, an opportunity that came his way when by chance he found a newspaper from the Himalayan Institute at the health club where he had been working.

"That's when I decided to go there," he says. "I wanted to immerse myself." At the Institute, he met Swami Rama, who taught him and encouraged him. "I wasn't focused on being skilled in the world," Smith says. "He put a stop to that." Swami urged him to balance spiritual pursuits with the ability to make a responsible living.

Yoga certainly fit in well with other aspects of Smith's life. Born in California and raised there and a number of other places, he had become a vegetarian in 1982 and was involved in the natural foods industry, working in and managing stores. All his training and interests knit together as he moved back and forth over a dozen years among jobs and cities, living in Minneapolis, New York, and Honesdale, teaching yoga, working in natural food stores, and doing a two-year stint in India with Swami Rama's hospital there. By 1997 he was in the Chicago area, assisting the director of the Himalayan Institute Midwest. He moved into that job when the director retired in 1999.

The holistic approach of the Himalayan Institute is a good fit for Smith. "Eating right, breathing, working with the mind, body, breath, emotions—to be successful on a spiritual path you have to bring all those things in," says Smith. "Yoga is the whole path."

Yoga is an unusual path for Smith, an African American man. Most of the yoga teachers who have been his colleagues—and many of his students—are middle-class white women. "That's been pretty much the profile," he says. Vegetarianism was close to a cultural aberration when he began that lifestyle practice in 1982. "That was a challenge," he recalls. "There were only a few of us."

Smith wishes that more of his African American brothers and sisters shared his interest in Eastern spirituality, but he understands why they are not so drawn to these meditative paths. African American spirituality expresses itself comfortably, he suggests, in the Protestant Christianity that historically has provided a faith home and cultural refuge. There is also less spiritual questing or faith-hopping in the community; faith is strong and tends to be traditional, with religious identification relatively fixed. "African Americans are more focused on what they've decided on spiritually, " Smith says. And Buddhism comes across as too elitist. "Buddhism wasn't [historically] for the masses," he says. Smith's own family was skeptical for a long time about his spiritual path, but is more accepting now that vegetarianism and yoga have become far more mainstream practices than they were twenty years ago, when he began moving in that spiritual direction.

Smith's own spiritual practice is multifaceted, including hatha yoga, meditation, attention to health, and *japa*, a practice of repeating one's own mantra. *Japa* is a technique for improving concentration and focusing the mind; it is also a devotion. Smith keeps a *mala*, a string of 108 beads, in his pocket at all times to help with his *japa*; the aim of the practice is to achieve a spontaneous, effortless repetition. "I try to integrate the viewpoint into my whole life, to be less self-oriented and see the bigger spiritual picture," he says.

Marian: "I think of myself as 'yoga'"

Marian, my meditation teacher, stuns me when she tells me her age. "I'll be seventy-six in November," she confesses. She could be taken for someone in her fifties. She's been practicing, and teaching, hatha yoga since 1972, and teaching meditation for ten years.

The first time Marian came to the Himalayan Institute was accidental, remarkable, and many years ago—about thirty in fact. She had accompanied a friend to yoga class, and the teacher waved her in. She remembers doing the plow, an inverted posture that stretches the back and enhances the flow of blood and oxygen throughout the body. At the time, Marian had recurring respiratory trouble, and would wake toward the end of the night, feeling congested. After that first yoga class, "The next morning I didn't wake up early," she says. "I was really surprised. So next week I went again, and again it happened with the plow. It was very specific."

With that as experiential proof, her thirty-year course of study began. At age seventy-five, she no longer feels the need to do hatha yoga each day as part of her routine, although she continues to do it two or three times weekly.

For Marian, the experience and benefits of what she does are both physical and spiritual, although spiritual growth was not part of her original intention. "In the beginning I really focused on the physical aspect, because that was so remarkable," she says. "There's no doubt the spiritual aspect was there and that I was ready for it, even though I didn't consciously look for it."

Raised a Roman Catholic, Marian had stopped attending church owing to her disagreement with some of the church's social stances. "Then yoga came along, and it was just the right fit," she says.

Marian met Himalayan Institute founder Swami Rama in 1972. At the time, the Institute was headquartered in the Chicago area, before it acquired its four-hundred-acre campus in Pennsylvania. He encouraged her involvement not only as a student but also as a volunteer at the center. She was there so much of the time, she says, that she eventually became involved in its administrative work as a volunteer. She also maintained her full-time job in a suburban library and found time to raise nine children. Her husband was uninterested in sharing her spiritual path, but, "He never objected," she says. "I was very, very lucky."

Marian considers her practice as her spiritual identity. "I never thought of it as Hindu," she says. "But I do think of myself as 'yoga.'"

Polly: "Yoga is what saved me"

Polly is another woman who was brought to yoga by health challenges. She had studied it on and off before taking it up more diligently in 1993 at the suggestion of a friend. She had back pains and the chronic tiredness that goes along with mothering two young children.

"That was the starting point," she says. Before going to bed at night, knowing she would be awakened by one or both restless young children, she would do at least twenty minutes of deep breathing. "I've often told people that yoga is what saved me," she says.

Her practice, and her spirituality, grew, leading to a change in her career. She moved from twenty years of involvement with theater, in which she had been directing shows and teaching acting, into healing. Polly, forty-three, is now a yoga teacher at the Himalayan Institute and a practitioner of *oshiatsu*, a particular kind of *shiatsu*, a Japanese healing practice and bodywork based on Chinese theories of energy centers.

"My concern is with healing and health and continuing to explore what it is to be a human being," she says. "It's been a natural progression on a spiritual path exploring how the spirit and mind affect the body."

Hatha yoga and breath exercises *(pranayama)* lead her quite naturally to a meditative state in which she can concentrate. "For me, even from the beginning, hatha practice was preparation for the meditation time," she says. "I found that doing hatha practice forced me into the one-point mind."

Polly's background and household is spiritually eclectic. Raised a Lutheran, she remembers attending Catholic churches frequently with relatives. "Something that was present, and I think I learned from my mother, was feeling comfortable worshiping anywhere. It didn't matter the denomination." Today, her husband is Jewish, and the family observes the Sabbath and attends synagogue. She also attends a Lutheran church with her children.

"There are certainly things I don't agree with in most organized religions, but that doesn't prevent me from being able to worship in a church," she says. "My yoga practice has only expanded my understanding of the Divine."

Glenn: "You have to change your whole life"

After years of thinking and reading about meditation and Eastern spirituality, Glenn, another student at the Himalayan Institute Midwest, finally decided to get serious.

"I would do breath practice and meditation practice on my own, but not real serious, not exact science," he explains. "About a year ago I finally, finally decided I was going to find a teacher."

And so over the past nine months he has taken every meditation class that the Institute has offered and made every session. He has been taking hatha yoga classes as well to help his posture and body. The results of his work have been quite apparent to him. "It's changed my life dramatically since I've gotten serious," he says emphatically and quickly. "It's made a great difference in my clarity and how I handle stress."

His job as co-owner of a large decorating firm is demanding. About thirty people work for him, half a dozen in the office and the rest in the field. Meditation keeps him calm, so he practices it every day.

Glenn's diligence was long in coming. Now forty-three, he first heard Institute founder Swami Rama speak almost thirty years ago. "When I was thirteen or fourteen, one of my friends took me to a seminar with Swami Rama," he recalls. That sparked an interest and he began reading widely, including books by Eastern-religions writer Alan Watts, anthropologist and shaman Carlos Castaneda, and mind-body specialist Deepak Chopra. "I never stopped studying," he says. One of his current favorite books is by Linda Johnsen, entitled *Meditation Is Boring?* (Himalyan Institute Press, 2000).

The change in his life has been fairly comprehensive. Glenn has become a complete vegan after twenty years of partial vegetarianism (although a traditional Hindu vegetarian diet does include some dairy products). He's been asked to train to be a teacher, but he is not sure, given his professional obligations, whether that's feasible for him now, or whether he's quite ready. "There's a lot I want to know before I do that," he says.

But after thirty years of sticking in a toe every so often, he's now reveling in the plunge. "I wanted something to happen for so long," he says. "I've known about it and know it takes time. For meditation to work, you have to change your whole life."

More Pathways

Many Westerners see Vedanta as the primary wisdom tradition of India, though it is but one of several Hindu philosophical systems. It might be defined as the essence of the Vedas, India's oldest and most sacred scriptures, said to have been revealed to ancient sages by divine inspiration. Many of the Vedas are concerned with priestly rites and rituals; the later Vedas, however—known as the Upanishads—emphasize the mystical paths to union with the Divine. It is these texts of "inner meaning" that are the basis of Vedanta philosophy. With its emphasis on the oneness of ultimate reality, its universalist approach to worship, and its meditative techniques of self-realization, Vedanta has attracted many American seekers.

In the late nineteenth and early twentieth centuries, Swami Vivekananda brought Vedanta to America. He was a delegate to the World Parliament of Religions, held in 1893 in Chicago. Swami Vivekananda's speech to the World Parliament was the first authentic presentation of India's religious tradition to Americans, and an eloquent one it was. Following the formal, scholarly speeches of other presenters, the swami won a standing ovation by warmly addressing the American audience as "brothers and sisters"—a dramatic expression of religious unity in action. The following year, Vivekananda established the Vedanta Society in New York City, and Vedantic philosophy began to attract many followers, including such well-known people as the writers Christopher Isherwood and Aldous Huxley.

Vivekananda himself was a student of the nineteenth-century Indian saint Sri Ramakrishna, a mystic and yogi who taught that all religions were paths to truth. Vedanta incorporates that view. Its core teachings hold that the real nature of humanity is divine, that the aim of human life is to realize this divine nature, and that all religions lead to the same truth: "Truth is one, though sages give it many names," proclaim the Vedas.

Given Vedanta's basic premises, meditation is a key tool in the realization of divinity. In *Meditation, Mind and Patanjali's Yoga*, Swami Bhaskarananda writes, "According to the sages, we should meditate in order to achieve the highest goal of human life—experiencing Divinity or the Ultimate Truth. It should be clearly understood that meditation or *dhyana* is only a means."

Vedanta centers are places where meditation is taught and practiced in the context of Vedantic teachings and the study of the work of Sri Ramakrishna and other influential Indian sages. The twelve Vedanta centers in the United States are homes for resident monks; Vedanta centers in India, known there as the Ramakrishna Mission, emphasize social service.

Chicago's Vedanta Society is especially historic, because Chicago was the place where the 1893 World Parliament of Religions was held. Vivekananda made his historic address at what is now the world-renowned Art Institute of Chicago. The portion of the city's famous Michigan Avenue that runs past the Art Institute has been renamed "Swami Vivekananda Way." In 1998, a ten-foot-tall bronze statue of Vivekananda was installed at the Hindu Temple of Greater Chicago. The local Vedanta society was established in 1930, and since 1967 has been at its present quarters in the cosmopolitan neighborhood that includes the University of Chicago. The current site includes a second, small building, which is a residence for women for short- or long-term stays. In 1971 ground was broken on an eighty-acre parcel of land in Ganges, Michigan, that now houses a temple, monastery, and retreat center. A children's camp is held there each summer. In June of 2001 the Ganges monastery was the site for a public conference on "Vedanta in the Third Millennium" that drew Vedanta swamis and hundreds of Vedantists from across the United States.

A statue in an alcove greets the visitor to the Vivekananda Vedanta Society in Chicago. What's surprising is that it's a statue of the Buddha. Vedantists are very inclusive. Sri Ramakrishna included Islamic practices in his life; he studied the life of Jesus and the Christian Bible.

The shrine room, for assemblies and meditation, holds pictures of Ramakrishna, Vivekananda, and Ramakrishna's wife, Sarada Devi, with whom he lived in a celibate marriage. She was his disciple and a teacher in her own right, revered by many as the "Holy Mother." Sarada Math, a monastic order for women in India, is named for her.

Also on display are pictures of Jesus and the Buddha. Flowers surround the photos; flowers are a customary and colorful offering of devotion in Hinduism. Symbols from many of the world's major religions are also visible on the walls: the Christian cross, the Muslim crescent and star, the Jewish Star of David, the Buddhist Wheel of Dharma.

Classes are held twice weekly on Vedanta philosophy and texts. Swami Chidananda, in his orange robe, leads Tuesday classes on the *Gospel of Sri Ramakrishna* (Ramakrishna Vivekananda Center, 1985), a biography and record of Ramakrishna's life compiled by one of his disciples. We open with a period of meditation; then Swami Chidananda offers a talk on the teachings of Ramakrishna.

The subject is religion—religion as a means of expressing the divine nature of one's self, part of the core belief that divine nature is indwelling and is our real nature. Real happiness, then, comes from the recognition of our innate divinity. A core teaching from the Upanishads is "That thou art" *(Tat tvam asi)*, meaning that you are one with the unlimited divinity of the Absolute. This realization also allows us to love everything in the world, because everything is part of the divine consciousness, which takes many particular and unique forms.

Religion is then the discipline for this realization, the means to the end. "Be practical, and practice it," Swami Chidananda says. "That's what

Sri Ramakrishna says." The class ends with meditative silence.

Balancing the

Under the watchful eye of an instructor, students perform the "sun salutation," a posture made up of twelve successive movements, in celebration of the sun's divinity and in preparation for hatha yoga (postures) and meditation. Hindu yoga and meditation centers take a holistic approach, incorporating both physical and mental exercises. Some U.S. centers embrace traditional aspects of Hinduism, including rituals and dress, while others dispense with these features of the Hindu religious tradition. (Photo: courtesy of the Sivananda

Brain

Following Ramakrishna's model, Jagdish, a teacher and clinical psychologist, maintains a very inclusive spiritual practice. A native of India who absorbed the core of Hinduism in his childhood, he also practices Buddhist insight meditation. "Truth is one, differently expressed by sages," Jagdish says, citing first in Sanskrit and then in English this often-quoted passage from the Vedas.

All of Jagdish's early education in India was family based. With many generations of teachers in his family, there was naturally an emphasis on learning, especially oral tradition. "I learned many things about meditation and holistic health even before I knew about meditation or yoga," he explains. "It's like breathing air without knowing what air is." His later formal education included the study of Sanskrit; he eventually became a teacher of Sanskrit and could read the scriptures of Hinduism in their original language.

Jagdish had another powerful spiritual influence. His father was a principal at a school visited in 1925 by the sage and political leader Mahatma Gandhi. Jagdish tells this story: "The first question he asked my father was, 'Where is your wife?' My father told him she was pregnant and couldn't make it. So Gandhi came to visit my home and blessed my mother. I was born the next day: May 15, 1925."

Their paths crossed again four years later, when the family lived across the river from the town where Gandhi had established his ashram. Young Jagdish and his father would attend evening meditation and prayers. "My father used to take me there, and I distinctly remember the presence of [Gandhi's] being, even if I didn't understand the words. I was only four."

Jagdish came to the United States in 1959 as a Fulbright scholar and acquired a master's degree and a doctorate from the University of Chicago—intellectual training that was different from his Indian upbringing and education. "I became more 'left-brained' in the United States," he says with a laugh, referring to the side of the brain associated with analytical thinking. The balance he finally sought between the right and left brains and their respective skills—between Eastern and Western knowledge—came to him through the practice of yoga and meditation, he says.

"Yoga is the cessation of the activities of the mind," he says. "Meditation is a process in which we really learn how to make the mind one-pointed. Different techniques are used to help the mind become one-pointed."

This understanding and practice fit well in what he knows spiritually and professionally about mind-body relationships. A practicing psychotherapist, he teaches his clients yoga meditation; he also teaches it in holistic health and psychology classes.

"This whole technique of meditation helps people to become more conflict-free and experience wholeness or balance or harmony," he continues. "That's the definition of yoga: It makes *us* united—all the dimensions of the being work in harmony."

He stresses the importance of disciplined daily practice. "It's a process," Jagdish says. "As I'm going through the process I have glimpses [of the goal]. But the path is the goal."

Buddhist meditation is a very useful alternative for him, depending on his need or frame of mind. The two meditation styles are different, he finds. In contrast to the one-pointed mind that yoga meditation develops, Buddhist insight meditation is much more open-ended and has helped him cultivate many levels of mindfulness.

"Mindfulness of all levels without judging or running away or getting attached to them is very helpful for me in meditation," Jagdish says. "Beyond the ego there is real awakening, or *bodhi*."

His interest in Buddhism sprang from a profound spiritual experience he had in 1959, around the time of year when Buddha's birthday is celebrated as a holiday. "As the day came closer, I had a vision or dream or altered consciousness in which I felt Buddha's presence," he says. A poem also came to him, and he wrote it down just as the parts occurred to him, in Sanskrit and Pali, languages of the Buddha's time, and Gujarati, Jagdish's native language. The poem explored his relationship and identification with the Buddha.

"His quest became my quest," Jagdish says. And so he learned more, especially from the teachings of S. N. Goenka, an Indian who studied in Burma and subsequently became one of the key teachers of insight meditation. Knowing as much as he did and having a deep and abiding interest in mind-body knowledge, it became obvious that he could learn and study more. So at the age of sixty-three, he enrolled for a second doctoral degree at the Illinois School of Professional Psychology in order to work more systematically to bring together knowledge and techniques from East and West.

"I was the oldest student in class," says Jagdish, who is now seventy-six and semi-retired from his teaching position. He devised his own synthesis of yoga and insight meditation, called integrative meditation, and taught it to subjects with cardiovascular problems. He then measured differences after eight weeks of practice, using the biological measures of blood pressure and heart rate, and the psychological measures of anger and anxiety. The results were interesting enough to convince him of the value of this integrative approach, with its universal spiritual foundation for understanding body-mind-spirit.

His own meditation practice comes to him as a daily surprise. "Every morning when I meditate, whatever comes is a gift," says Jagdish. "It has helped me relate to life more openly, welcoming the gifts I really need."

Steps for Beginners

- Understand the breadth of yoga. Yoga in its fullest sense is a mind-body-spirit discipline. It encompasses body movement, diet, breathing practice and awareness, meditation, and a number of other practices, all designed to work together to the spiritual end of enlightenment. As Indians understand it, four different kinds of yoga can lead to God.

  Americans generally use and understand the term *yoga* in the narrower sense of systematic stretching exercises and postures for the body. This type of yoga is usually hatha yoga. Americanized systems such as "power yoga" are based on the original Indian teachings and poses. All yogas, whether taught at the local park district or an ashram, share a holistic view of human capacities.

- Appreciate the breadth of the religious context and original meaning of yoga. Hinduism is a vastly detailed religion, with cosmology, history, worship, and a pantheon of deities that are expressions of an underlying divine unity—"Truth is one," as the Vedas say. It has a long history, the world's oldest body of scripture, and roughly eight hundred million contemporary practitioners in what many say is the world's most devout nation. Hatha yoga and meditation are practices within this vast religion, which will ultimately lead the practitioner to liberation *(moksha)*.

- Know your expectations. Yoga is not a fast track; it is a thorough and subtle track that can knit the pieces of the day together with the touchstone of breath awareness, long after a quiet morning meditation is over. Its physical component makes it especially suited to certain types of active people.

For thousands of years, yoga meditation has been the way to know God, as the sage Patanjali said. Today, the way of yoga presents traditional Eastern wisdom in forms that are accessible to Americans. Swami Rama says, "From silence emanate happiness, peace and bliss.... That is the final goal of meditation."

Selected Resources

Books

Bhaskarananda, Swami. *Meditation, Mind and Patanjali's Yoga: A Practical Guide to Spiritual Growth for Everyone.* Seattle: Viveka Press, 2001.

Cope, Stephen. *Yoga and the Quest for the True Self.* New York: Bantam Doubleday Dell, 1999.

Frawley, David. *Vedantic Meditation: Lighting the Flame of Awareness.* Berkeley, Calif.: North Atlantic Books, 2000.

Iyengar, B. K. S. *The Tree of Yoga.* Boston: Shambhala, 1989.

Lasater, Judith. *Living Your Yoga: Finding the Spiritual in Everyday Life.* Berkeley, Calif.: Rodmell Press, 2000.

Prabhavananda, Swami, and Christopher Isherwood, trans. *How to Know God: The Yoga Aphorisms of Patanjali.* Hollywood, Calif.: Vedanta Press, 1996.

Rama, Swami. *Meditation and Its Practice.* Honesdale, Pa.: Himalayan Institute Press, 1992.

Sivananda Yoga Vedanta Center. *Yoga Mind and Body (DK Living).* London and New York: Dorling Kindersley, 1998.

Vivekananda, Swami. *Meditation and Its Methods.* Edited by Swami Chetanananda. Hollywood, Calif.: Vedanta Press, 1978.

Yogananda, Paramahansa. *The Autobiography of a Yogi.* Los Angeles: Self-Realization Fellowship, 1979.

Centers and organizations

Himalayan International Institute of Yoga Science and Philosophy
RR 1, Box 400
Honesdale, PA 18431
800-822-4547 or 570-253-5551
www.HimalayanInstitute.org

Kripalu Center for Yoga & Health
P.O. Box 793
Route 183
Lenox, MA 01240-0793
800-741-7353 (out of state)
413-448-3152 (within state)
www.kripalu.org

Vivekananda Vedanta Society
5423 South Hyde Park Boulevard
Chicago, IL 60615
773-363-0027
www.vedantasociety-chicago.org

Internet sites

- www.hinduismtoday.com—A readable guide to contemporary Hindu expression, with emphasis on spirituality.

- www.hindunet.org—"The Hindu Universe," with comprehensive information about religion and spirituality.

- www.sivananda.org—A worldwide network of yoga spirituality centers and ashrams.

- www.sivanandadlshq.org/home.html—The Divine Life Society, the wellspring of the Sivananda group, with excellent and comprehensive links.

- www.vedanta.com—Information about Vedanta philosophy, and publications of Vedanta Press.

6

Sufi Meditation: Remembering the Beloved

This longing
you express is *the return message.*
The grief you cry out from
draws you toward union.

JALALUDDIN RUMI, "LOVE DOGS,"
IN *THE ESSENTIAL RUMI*

A Call to Prayer

Although I have traveled to the commercial northwest side of Chicago, an area filled with aging small shops and warehouses with corrugated siding, entering this storefront ushers me into a different world. Inside, the floor is covered with large, thick prayer rugs. Men and women—black, brown, and white people, from old men with white hair and beards to a tiny dark-haired infant no more than a month old—gradually assemble, sorting themselves into separate seating areas.

All the women wear loose-fitting clothing and scarves that cover their hair. A few of the men also have their heads covered with a turban in the style that the Prophet Muhammad is believed to have worn. Yards of lightweight fabric are wrapped round a small pointed cap that can be seen underneath the turban; the fabric is tied so that a small tail extends down from the headpiece. Everyone leaves their shoes at the door; a few people wear traditional leather prayer slippers, which are thin, soleless, and wrap the ankle, bootlike.

Then the traditional call to prayer is chanted in Arabic. Though the chanter is not a muezzin calling from a tower across the streets of the town, his call nonetheless signals to us sitting inside the Chicago storefront that the service, a remembrance of God—*dhikr Allah*—liturgy based on a form first used a thousand years ago by Central Asian Naqshbandi Sufi masters, is about to begin.

The dhikr liturgy involves both leader and group. The *imam*, or prayer leader, Abdul Haqq offers supplications, and the assembly follows with chanted prayers. The prayers invoke the name of God, and they are short and repetitive because their function is to repeat God's name. In Islam, God has ninety-nine names, which reveal God to be, among other qualities, merciful, tender, gracious, and just; these attributes are also to be repeated. The repetition of *Allah*, the Arabic word for "God," is the heart of the dhikr, almost literally. Repeated with crescendoing force, it is intended to suggest the human heartbeat, the heartbeat of the universe.

Remembering God

Hidden in hearts and behind doors, Sufism—generally defined as the mystical aspect of Islam—is around us. God, and how to experience God directly and remember God constantly, are at the heart of the beliefs and practices of Sufis. Sufism is a surrender—the term *islam* literally means "surrender"—of the heart, in which God is often portrayed as the beloved, indicative of the depth of the Sufi seeker's longing for union with the Divine. All Muslims express surrender to God through the distinctive prostrations that accompany their prayers. Touching forehead to ground during the prescribed five daily prayer times is a powerful and repeated reminder of the insignificance of individual ego.

Dhikr (pronounced *zikr* in English) is a mystical approach to God. Dhikr is remembrance of God (Allah), and often consists of the repetition of God's name in a variety of ways and contexts. Remembrance of God is important, and for the Sufi is as essential as the lover remembering the beloved.

When humans forget God, they sin. Adam and Eve forgot God; in going against God's directive, they forgot God's words, they forgot God's will. In the Qur'an, Islam's scripture, God also promises to remember those who remember. Repeating God's name in dhikr is a basic expression of remembrance of the Divine.

Dhikr can be silent or vocal, private or shared by a group. Sometimes dhikr can be done in conjunction with breathing exercises, movements, or other practices intended to disrupt normal consciousness and tear away some of the seventy thousand veils between the seeker and the beloved.

Many Sufis think of dhikr as a practice of the heart, not merely of the lips. "When you hear a song and can't get it out of your head, it's like that," says Patrick, a Sufi and follower of Sri Lankan teacher Muhammed Raheem Bawa Muhaiyaddeen. "Silent dhikr, within you— you can *do* it or *be* it, however you look at it."

Who Is a Sufi?

Dhikr can be described as "Sufi meditation," but not all Sufis would assent to that description. Sufism encompasses a wide range of orders— groups that descend from different masters of the spiritual tradition— and interpretations. Those who call themselves Sufi can disagree about who else may be called a Sufi. Appreciating these differences becomes essential early on in one's exposure to Sufism.

While Sufism is often thought of as the mystical aspect of Islam, Sufis differ on how much Islamic practice must be taught and followed. Not all Sufis are primarily Islamic; adherents of universalist, or Western, Sufism emphasize the aspects of universalism and unity in which Islam is rich. Hazrat Inayat Khan, who introduced Sufism to audiences in the United States and Europe between 1910 and 1926, said, "Sufism existed before Mohammed, before Jesus Christ, before Abraham. It is true that the mystics in the world of Islam are Sufis, but that does not mean that Sufi means the mystic of Islam. For instance, the green color is the national color of the Irish, but that does not mean that everybody who dresses in green is from Ireland."

More traditional Sufis are sometimes skeptical of universalist Sufism, which they tend to regard as "New Age." These traditionalists maintain the required five practices—pillars—of Islam that define a Muslim, among which is prayer—*salat*, prescribed five times a day. Even within Islamic or traditional Sufism, however, there are many Sufi orders, each with different founding teachers. And the matter of labeling grows even more complex within the larger context of Islam. Not all Muslims accept Sufism as a legitimate aspect of their religion, in much the same way that some Christians cast a cold eye on the mystical teachings within Christianity. During its history, Sufism has occasionally encountered persecution from authorities who saw it as unorthodox practice. And Islam itself is hardly monolithic, having spread over the course of fourteen centuries to dozens of countries and cultures, and having been shaped by hundreds of significant spiritual teachers.

The Naqshbandi Sufi order is one of forty traditional orders of Sufism within Islam; these orders have different branches, further multiplying Sufi groups. The Haqqani branch of the Naqshbandi is traditional in observances and ways. Members are strict about keeping *shariah*, the Muslim code of behavior based upon the words, customs, and practices of the Prophet Muhammad. Hence, dressing in traditional fashion may be viewed as one way of approximating the practices and habits of Muhammad, the perfect exemplar of the right human relationship to God and, therefore, an excellent model of how to live one's life.

The Naqshbandi may hearken to ancient Middle Eastern and Central Asian roots, but they are also American. Laleh, who is a writer, publisher, and psychologist, tells me that the Chicago gathering attracts a lot of people whose Arabic is limited; virtually all the thirty or so in attendance are either converted Americans or first-generation Americans descended from traditional Muslim cultures. Even the *shaykh*—the teacher and prayer leader—himself is American, despite his Arabic name, Abdul Haqq (*haqq* means "truth"). He converted in 1978.

Another traditional Sufi group was started by a Sri Lankan, but it is based in America and has branches around the world. The Bawa Muhaiyaddeen Fellowship in Philadelphia grew up around the teacher of the same name, who came to this country in 1971 from his native Sri Lanka.

Carolyn was a student of his even before he came to the United States. "He was here three months and word got out and a lot of people showed up and never left," she says. Over time, a residential community of followers grew up at the edge of Philadelphia. Followers of M. R. Bawa Muhaiyaddeen also keep Islamic law, custom, and practices. These Sufis may begin the day with dhikr at 4:30 A.M. in the stately tomb of their teacher, who died in 1986 and is interred in a large traditional structure that functions as both tomb and shrine.

The Drop and the Ocean

As in other esoteric and mystical traditions, metaphoric speech is common in Sufism. The work of the thirteenth-century Turkish poet Jalaluddin Rumi, currently the best-selling poet in the United States, is a rich body of elaborate metaphor, using the conceits of earthly love to describe vividly the longing of the Sufi for the beloved, God. That longing,

Sufis teach, is itself the way to God. Sufis also like to use the metaphor of the drop of water. When it falls into the ocean, it is no longer a separate drop. The ocean represents union with God.

What gets in the way of union with God is ego, which separates the soul from God. Sufism seeks the annihilation of the ego, a state of consciousness called *fana*, in which the "I" is gone and can instead be filled with God. In this way, the lover—the believer—submits to God.

It is also important to submit to the guidance of a teacher, a *shaykh*. Ninth-century Sufi mystic Bayazid Bistami said: "One who has no master has Satan for a leader." In *The Shambhala Guide to Sufism*, scholar Carl Ernst writes, "It is hard to overestimate the importance of the master-disciple relationship in Sufism."

About her teacher M. R. Bawa Muhaiyaddeen, Carolyn says, "Everybody was very committed to Bawa. He was unlike anybody else any of us had ever seen."

Walking the Sufi Path: Stories from Practitioners

Patrick: "Your life is remembering"

Patrick formally began his spiritual journey in the 1960s, when he was in a Franciscan seminary, a candidate for ordination to the priesthood in the Roman Catholic Church. He thinks of Francis of Assisi, founder of the order, as a kind of mystic. "Francis used Jesus as his inner guide," Patrick says. "A Sufi might use both the Prophet and Jesus." Patrick wanted to talk about mysticism; his superiors most definitely did not. And so he decided to leave, and spent a few years thereafter studying spiritualities, at a time when interest in the spiritual traditions and teachers of the East was blossoming, and when a variety of gurus came to visit America. He looked into Hinduism, visited with Sikhs. It was his Sikh friends who told him about a teacher from Sri Lanka.

Patrick remembers vividly the first time he encountered information about the Sufi master. He walked into a room in Woodstock, New York, one day in 1973 and found a Chinese man meditating in front of a TV screen. The man, without moving, told him to look on the table, where a pamphlet entitled "Who Is God?" lay. The pamphlet was modest, eight pages, and typed.

"I was intrigued," recalls Patrick. "'Who is God?' I had studied that question all my life. I remember sitting down and reading it. I disappeared for about two hours, and then I came to. As soon as I finished the last word, I said, 'I have to go see this guy.'"

Patrick did, and the connection was swift and apparent. "[He] immediately took me as a student. It was immediately personal, not magical—he simply seemed to know what I was there for and didn't ask me a lot of questions."

Patrick, fifty-five, has now been a student of M. R. Bawa Muhaiyaddeen's teachings for twenty-eight years. "The answer eventually came. Now I work on the rest of it."

His work is constant remembering of God—dhikr that is a part of being itself, that is on the breath and in the blood and annihilates the self because "Only you, O God, are," explains Patrick, who today also uses the name Muhammad. "When dhikr is constant, when you go beyond the breath level, when you get to the blood and nervous system level and everything that's flowing within you, then your life is remembering. Everything within you remembers God. When every aspect of your physical being is remembering, you can't forget."

Laleh: "Sufism is a lifelong process"
Laleh has a Ph.D. in counseling psychology in addition to two master's degrees. She has traveled the world as a translator for members of the Iranian parliament, and published a magazine for women in Iran. Her publications include a hefty work on Islamic law, and works on the his-

tory of Sufism, Islam, and women in Sufism. Laleh decided she was ready to make the commitment to adopt modest dress when she was living and working in Iran. "Everyone needs to make this decision personally," she says.

Laleh was born in Iran, the child of an American nurse and an Iranian doctor. She was raised in America, though unintentionally at the outset. While still an infant, she returned to this country with her mother when her grandfather, her mother's father, became ill in 1939. Then World War II broke out, making it impossible for Laleh and her family to return to Iran until 1945. Laleh's parents subsequently divorced, and her mother returned to America once again with Laleh and her six brothers and sisters, so the children could receive an American education.

Growing up, Laleh attended a Catholic school, and she decided she didn't want to be left out. "Every Friday, Sister would say, 'Who's going to communion?' I came home and said, 'I want to become Catholic.'" She did, with her mother's permission, but eventually found herself in disagreement with the church. After college, she married an Iranian man who had grown up in the United States, and returned with him to Iran. There she met the man who would become her teacher, the Islamic scholar and Sufi expert Seyyed Hossein Nasr. "He told me, 'Since your father is Muslim, you're considered to be Muslim.' I said, 'I don't know anything about Islam,' and he said, 'Learn.' That's when I started my journey. I was twenty-four."

In Iran, Laleh worked as a translator. She also wrote in English on Sufi history, since her degree was in history. She and her husband divorced, and she returned to the United States in 1988, following the last of her three adult children to Albuquerque, New Mexico. There, she returned to school, studying graduate-level psychology. She was Iranian and Sufi—two identities that the people she was meeting either didn't know about or didn't want to know about.

"I hadn't been in America for twenty years," she recalls. "Nobody wanted to talk about Iran or hear about Sufism. I was feeling kind of isolated." One day, as she was leaving the classroom, her professor called her attention to a method of counseling with Sufi origins, suggesting she might want to study it. It was the enneagram, a traditional theory of personality based on a system of types.

A path opened with sudden clarity, and she knew just what to do: She would pursue the enneagram professionally, and actively study and practice Sufism. She was initiated into the Nimatullahi order, which was well established in Iran and therefore familiar to her. When she ended up in Chicago professionally, she found it difficult to attend Nimatullahi gatherings. Then she met the Naqshbandi-Haqqani leader in America, Shaykh Muhammad Hisham Kabbani. Laleh was permitted to become a Naqshbandi initiate also, and she has been a practicing Naqshbandi for the past seven years.

For Laleh, Sufism is a lifelong moral and spiritual path with an end-point that constantly recedes. "You never really *become* a Sufi," she explains. "You're on the path, in the process. Sufism is a lifelong process of inner development and self-purification."

Sufism offers her a profound way of uniting psychology with spirituality, bringing together her professional and personal interests. Spiritual development can be understood in psychological terms. Sufis strive for personal change, the development of virtue, and the moderation of both reason and passion so that the world of intuition can be entered when the seeker is ready.

"I don't know what you're supposed to feel like in spiritual development," she continues. "I'm still working on it. Work with the Sufi enneagram has shown me that until a person leaves aside negative vices and develops virtue, you're not into spirituality in the sense of experiencing it."

Laleh feels that non-Islamic Sufism is not deep enough for her, but she can't dismiss its validity for others. "There are so many ways to God. Who am I to say, 'This isn't the way'?" she asks.

Seeing in a New Light

"Meditation could in fact be defined as the art of modulating consciousness," writes Pir Vilayat Inayat Khan in *Awakening: A Sufi Experience*. God consciousness is what members of the Sufi Order International, formerly known as Sufi Order of the West, seek to recognize and develop.

Kashfinur tells me that one can *talk* about Sufism, but it is really a path of experience. Like all good mystics, Sufis can be found on the other side of words, "in ecstasy in God's company," as Kashfinur says.

Kashfinur is the Chicago-area teacher of followers of Hazrat Inayat Khan and his son, Pir Vilayat Inayat Khan. Hazrat Inayat Khan, an initiate of the Chishti order of Sufism in India, was a gifted musician who brought Indian music as well as Sufism to the West when he came to the United States in 1910. Inayat Khan returned to India in 1926, and died there at the age of forty-four in 1927; his son succeeded him as spiritual head of the order. In February of 2000, the leadership of the Sufi Order International in North America was vested in Pir Zia Inayat Khan, eldest son of, and the eventual spiritual successor to, Pir Vilayat Inayat Khan.

Hazrat Inayat Khan's first book written in the West, *A Sufi Message of Spiritual Liberty*, published in 1914 by the Theosophical Publishing Society, opens with these words in its preface: "Sufism is a religious philosophy of love, harmony and beauty." This philosophy is incorporated in the prayers and practices of the Sufi Order International.

If this kind of Sufism is aesthetic and ecstatic, it is also esoteric. As in other meditative and mystic traditions, some things aren't open to beginners; some things don't get talked about, because words aren't the appropriate medium, and certain truths are best left unsaid. Sufi scholar

Carl Ernst writes, "The basic esotericism of Sufism rested on the principle that only certain qualified people would be able to understand and experience the highest spiritual truths. Therefore, to blurt out something revealing one's intimate experience with God was rash, to say the least."

Kashfinur puts it more simply. "Talking is filling space," he says, acknowledging a modern American proclivity toward verbal communication.

Kashfinur, who uses his spiritual name legally, is a Westerner. He has lived and traveled around the globe, including India, Tibet, and the Middle East. He was born in Prague of German parents during World War II. He tells the story of his spiritual life with some reticence—not wanting to fill too much space—saying only that he first encountered Sufism "through crisis."

"I became aware," he narrates, "that there was more than just this being. At a party, there was an interesting, beautiful face. I was forty then."

A door of opportunity and interest opened. He remembers visiting a Sufi camp in New York where there were families with children. He had no children; he didn't even like them at the time. But something struck him. He could tell by the behavior of the children, and parents toward the children, that they were following a spiritual path. "It was the beauty of the children," he says. At the camp, he met influential Sufi teachers.

Kashfinur subsequently left the United States for Belgium. He studied with Pir Vilayat Inayat Khan. "He asked me to start a center" in the Chicago area, Kashfinur says. Kashfinur had not wanted to return to the area; he had already lived there doing a postdoctoral fellowship in virology at the University of Chicago and was not eager to return. But a major employer was wooing him, bringing opportunities together. He decided to take the job, with a pharmaceutical firm, and has now worked there as a research scientist for twenty years; he has also been practicing as a Sufi and Sufi teacher.

The Sufi group that he leads meets monthly. On occasion they will conduct a Universal Worship service, which includes readings from the scriptures of the major religious traditions. Beyond its purpose of bringing people together to worship the God of all, the Universal Worship service encourages people "to get more insight into different religions and respect each other more," explains Kashfinur, who is a *cherag*, an ordained minister qualified to lead the service. "If you see the unity behind everything, how can you not respect everything?"

Meditation as this order practices it may involve breath, visualization, movement, chanting, and other techniques drawing on body and mind faculties. Purification is an important process of spiritual growth; Sufis think of it as cleaning out the heart for God. It also relates to the intention of Sufism itself. Although there is some disagreement over exactly how the term was derived, one explanation links the etymology of *Sufi* to *suf*, the Arabic word for "wool." The earliest Sufis wore woolen garments to distinguish themselves from their silk-wearing counterparts, whom they considered too worldly. Sufism itself represents an attempt to practice "pure" Islam, an Islam of meaning rather than form, of heart and intention rather than rote performance of prescribed religious duties. Another etymology connects *Sufi* to *safa*, meaning "purity"; still another to *sophia*, meaning "wisdom" in Greek.

The Practice of Purification

Kashfinur shows me the practice of elemental purification breaths, a good starting point for meditation. Here, as in so many schools, breath is key: it is a practice, a substance in itself, a door to, in Pir Vilayat's words, "modulating consciousness." The breathing practice can be done standing or seated, and it helps achieve greater attunement with the four traditional elements of earth, water, fire, and air. Concentration stays with the breath.

Purification of the earth element is first. The meditator exhales, imagining that spent elements and impurities, such as the carbon dioxide gas our lungs expel, are being drawn away through the soles of the feet into an absorbent earth. Inhalation draws fresh vitality and energy in from the physical environment. Inhalation and exhalation are done through the nose.

Water purification is done by inhalation through the nose and exhalation through the mouth. Exhalation brings a sense of cooling, like a shower of purifying water. Inhalation is visualized as the flow of pure water, again refreshing and cleansing.

Fire purification requires inhalation through the mouth, exhalation through the nose. With each inhalation the meditator imagines a fire rising along a central internal axis, like that present in the Indian system of *chakras*, or energy centers. Inhalation and exhalation work to transform this central fire to light, radiating from the heart center of energy and producing a sense of a shower of light.

Air purification takes place by inhalation and exhalation through the mouth. The air purification is considered liberating, freeing the meditator to soar toward divine consciousness and away from the bondage of ego.

The purification breathing settles the mind and mobilizes the subtle internal energy that the meditation process can harness in pursuit of divine union, the Sufi goal. Sufi meditation also makes use of the imagery and visualization of light and qualities of light, including its different colors, in other practices. "We are to God as the rays are to the sun," says Kashfinur.

The separation of individual human from God is conceptual and illusory, and the way to God consists of experiencing the removal of illusory separation. The longing for God points the way to follow. "You want to become one with your beloved," Kashfinur says. Seeing through the separation is what Islam teaches at its core: *la ilaha illa 'llah*. This is the most frequent utterance of any Muslim, and is to be constantly on the lips. Non-Sufi Muslims understand it to mean, "There is no god but

God"; this is the central confession of Islam. Sufis understand the assertion to mean, "There is *nothing* but God," a mystical statement that might puzzle or even affront the pious but nonmystic believer. It is the quintessential Sufi view.

Verena is a member of the Sufi group that Kashfinur leads. She is also an active participant in the Dances of Universal Peace; a dance circle meets monthly in the Chicago area. She remembers "years and years ago" attending a workshop on finding the soul's purpose.

"The way they opened it, they did some Sufi dancing and it was just wonderful," she says. "It opened people to each other." She wanted to follow up, but no door opened until she encountered the book *Prayers of the Cosmos: Meditations on the Aramaic Words of Jesus,* by Neil Douglas-Klotz (Harper San Francisco, 1994), a Sufi who has done extensive work translating the original Aramaic words of Jesus. Tucked inside the book like an unexpected invitation was a flyer for a Dances of Universal Peace camp in the Chicago area. She called immediately, but it was too late. The following summer, however, she was there, and for several summers following, through the 1980s.

"It was an unbelievable spiritual experience," she says. "I was floating all the time, and then came down to earth and realized it was a very deep spiritual path." The dances that affected her most powerfully were drawn from Sufism. That eventually led her to Kashfinur's Sufi meditation group.

The monthly meeting of Kashfinur's group lasts all day and includes prayers, chanting, meditation, breathing awareness, and a shared meal. Chanting uses the ninety-nine beautiful names of God from the Islamic tradition, chanted first aloud and then silently. Eventually, even the silent chant ceases, and then the Sufi holds the names of God wordlessly in his or her heart. These names are archetypal qualities that the Divine Being expresses through the creation, such as compassion, peace, and sovereignty.

"It's really powerful, and you can feel the energy," says Verena. She continues with the dance group as well as the Sufi group. "I think it keeps me alive," she says.

Verena is seventy-four, and was brought up in Switzerland in Zwingli Protestantism, then lived in Germany and attended the Lutheran church. "I'm still a Christian," she says, "but I don't look on Christ as being the only one."

Other Orders

Like Islamic Sufism, Sufism in the United States is organized into different groups. The order established by Hazrat Inayat Khan and his succession, the Sufi Order International, has a number of branches and centers, including the community known as The Abode of the Message, in New Lebanon, New York, where Pir Zia Inayat Khan lives.

Followers of Hazrat Inayat Khan included an American named Samuel Lewis, known also as Sufi SAM, from Sufi Ahmed Murad, his spiritual name. Lewis was also a student of the Rinzai Zen Buddhist school and of dancer Ruth St. Denis; in San Francisco in the late 1960s he began to teach a practice of dancing now known as the Dances of Universal Peace. The Dances are based not only on Sufi music, but also on movement and chant from other spiritual traditions. Founded in 1982, the International Network for the Dances of Universal Peace is now an independent worldwide organization promoting the Dances and training teachers. The followers of Sufi SAM make up the Sufi Islamia Ruhaniat Society. Other Western Sufi groups, and leaders, also exist.

Khadija: "looking for the heart path"
Khadija, fifty-four, a former Midwesterner now living in the San Francisco Bay area, is an American Sufi who belongs to the Ruhaniat Society. She has been practicing Sufism for ten years and attends group dhikr regularly. Her own practice of dhikr can regularly lead her to deep inter-

nal silence. "I'm in a wordless state and I'm busy doing whatever the group is doing, but there's a quality of depth and emptiness that is precious," she says.

Her practice also includes dancing; dance circles are relatively easy to find in the Bay Area. Usually done in a circle and sometimes with partners, dancing helps a Sufi seeker begin to experience the frame of mind and being that dhikr expresses and cultivates. "The dances will show a seeker a kinesthetic and transpersonal path in relating to other people," she explains. "Dhikr refines the vocabulary and depth, is more profound and internal and personal. At dhikr, some people are so inner you can't tell what they're doing."

Seeking her spiritual path, Khadija had practiced in other traditions, including Quakerism, with its practice of silent meeting for worship.

Dance can provide a gateway through which the Divine and human meet. In Sufism, the dancer receives energy from God with her right hand turned toward heaven, and she returns energy to the earth through her left hand. (Photo: Jennifer J. Wilson. Reprinted from Praying with Our Hands: Twenty-One Practices of Embodied Prayer from the World's Spiritual Traditions, *SkyLight Paths, 2000.)*

She now practices some Buddhist meditation in addition to Sufism. Sufism appeals to her because of its connection to music, and because it is so body-based rather than intellectual.

Echoing Sufis of other schools, she says, "I was looking for a heart path."

Steps for Beginners

A little sorting out helps. Like so many spiritual traditions, Sufism encompasses a great variety of paths within itself. It can be Islamic or universalist. From either side of that basic divide, teachers and orders branch out. As in Buddhism, teachers try to trace their lineage back to the order founder and ultimately back to the Prophet Muhammad, a chain of authority called *silsila*. Ernst writes, "The symbolic importance of these lineages was immense; they provided a channel to divine authority through the horizontal medium of tradition."

Let a teacher lead. In addition to its development within many different schools, Sufism is by definition esoteric. Because of that, it is best learned through a teacher and in the context of a group of practitioners. This can take some hunting. Sufism is not as well established in this country as the religious traditions of Asia, making reliable sources of information less available. Sufi communities themselves are also fewer in number and farther apart.

Hunt for resources. Reading has been a point of entry for many Americans into meditative spiritual traditions. Not surprisingly, Sufi texts are also harder to find in general bookstores, although specialty sources exist. (See the resource list at the end of the chapter.) One source of information is growing, however: the Internet. Many Sufi orders have established websites. The American Muslim community as a whole is increasing its presence in cyberspace in order to be able to tell its own story and link its communities—*ummah*, the Arabic word for the larger Muslim world—here and across the world.

▢ You might want to dance. Khadija, the Ruhaniat Sufi practitioner, says that dancing is an accessible entryway to this spirituality. Dancing introduces the themes that are the basis of dhikr meditation. "Dancing is a training ground for dhikr," she says. "Some dances will be fun, some will be deeper."

Parts of the rich history of Sufi culture also decisively shape the contemporary popular American understanding of Sufism. The Sufi poet Rumi is the best-selling poet in America, a phenomenon that has raised awareness of Sufism. Thanks to growing popular interest in world music, Sufi music and its distinctive vocalizing can readily be heard on movie soundtracks and compact discs. The whirling dervishes of Turkey, known for their ritual turning dance, are members of the Mevlevi Order, followers of the poet Rumi. Their whirling is an expression of *sama*—which literally means "listening"—a musical ritual that can produce ecstasy. Rumi's work and other examples of the richness of Islamic art, poetry, music, dance, and literature are door openers to Sufism for beginners, for those unaware of the centuries of mystical spiritual teaching and tradition that Islam has fostered.

Selected Resources

Books

Bakhtiar, Laleh. *Sufi Expressions of the Mystic Quest*. London and New York: Thames and Hudson, 1987.

Barks, Coleman, trans. *The Essential Rumi*. San Francisco: Harper San Francisco, 1995.

Bawa Muhaiyaddeen, M. R. *To Die Before Death: The Sufi Way of Life*. Philadelphia: Fellowship Press, 1997.

Ernst, Carl. *The Shambhala Guide to Sufism*. Boston: Shambhala, 1997.

Helminski, Kabir. *The Knowing Heart: A Sufi Path of Transformation*. Boston: Shambhala, 2000.

Inayat Khan, Hazrat. *The Art of Being and Becoming*. New Lebanon, N.Y.: Omega Publications, 1990.

Inayat Khan, Pir Vilayat. *Awakening: A Sufi Experience*. New York: Tarcher/Putnam, 1999.

———. *That Which Transpires behind That Which Appears*. New Lebanon, N.Y.: Omega Publications, 1994.

Inayat Khan, Pir Zia, ed. *A Pearl in Wine: Essays on the Life, Music and Sufism of Hazrat Inayat Khan*. New Lebanon, N.Y.: Omega Publications, 2001.

Nurbakhsh, Javad. *In the Tavern of Ruin: Seven Essays on Sufism*. London: Khaniqahi-Nimatullahi Publications, 1978.

Schimmel, Annemarie. *Mystical Dimensions of Islam*. Chapel Hill: University of North Carolina Press, 1985.

Shah, Idries. *The Sufis*. New York: Anchor, 1971.

Vaughan-Lee, Llewellyn. *Love Is a Fire: The Sufi's Mystical Journey Home*. Inverness, Calif.: Golden Sufi Publications, 2000.

———. *Sufism: Transformation of the Heart*. Inverness, Calif.: Golden Sufi Publications, 1995.

Centers and organizations

Bawa Muhaiyaddeen Fellowship
5820 Overbrook Avenue
Philadelphia, PA 19131-1221
215-879-6300
www.bmf.org

Golden Sufi Center
P.O. Box 428
Inverness, CA 94937-0427
415-663-8773
www.goldensufi.org

International Association of Sufism
14 Commercial Boulevard, Suite 101
Novato, CA 94949
415-472-6959
www.ias.org

International Network for the Dances of Universal Peace
P.O. Box 55994
Seattle, WA 98115
206-522-4353
www.dancesofuniversalpeace.org

Naqshbandi Sufi Way
17195 Silver Parkway #201
Fenton, MI 48430
810-593-1222
www.naqshbandi.org

Sufi Islamia Ruhaniat Society
P.O. Box 51118
Eugene, OR 97405
541-345-5223
www.ruhaniat.org

Sufi Order International
North American Secretariat
P.O. Box 30065
Seattle, WA 98103
206-525-6992
www.sufiorder.org

The Threshold Society
151 Emerald City Way
Watsonville, CA 95076
861-685-3995
www.sufism.org

Internet sites

- www.arches.uga.edu/~godlas/Sufism.html—Sufism, Sufis, and Sufi Orders: Sufism's Many Paths, an accessible and knowledgeable guide to Sufi background and Sufi orders.

- www.nimatullahi.org/KN.HTM—The Nimatullahi Sufi Order.

Other sources of information

Islamic Texts Society/Fons Vitae
49 Mockingbird Valley Drive
Louisville, KY 40207-1366
502-897-3641
www.fonsvitae.com
(A nonprofit, charitable foundation devoted to making available works from the world's great spiritual traditions, especially Sufism.)

Kazi Publications
3023 West Belmont Avenue
Chicago, IL 60618
773-267-7001
www.kazi.org
(A nonprofit organization that is the oldest and largest Muslim publisher and distributor of books on Islam in North America.)

Wisdom's Child
256 Darrow Road
New Lebanon, NY 12125-2615
518-794-8181
www.wisdomschild.com
(A bookstore devoted to Sufism.)

7

Jewish Meditation: Awakening to Tradition

We now know that there was a vibrant Jewish mystical community in second- and third-century Palestine. Through meditative techniques and devotions, these seekers tried to ascend through the palaces (or Heikhalot) of heaven, hoping ultimately to behold God.

LAWRENCE KUSHNER, *THE WAY INTO JEWISH MYSTICAL TRADITION* (JEWISH LIGHTS, 2001)

Midnight: A Time to Experience the Presence of God

The houses I pass by are dark because the people inside them are sleeping. The lights of stores are out, their parking lots empty. It's well past everybody's closing time.

Traffic on the highways is blessedly light, so it's easy to be fleet. Near midnight is a good time to travel, and it's also a good time to meditate. The lights are on inside Bene Shalom, a Jewish temple in the northern-Chicago suburb of Skokie. The temple is hosting one of its regular midnight meditation gatherings.

Midnight is thought to be a sacred time, explains Rabbi Douglas

163

Goldhamer, the temple's rabbi. Within the Jewish mystical tradition, midnight and the time that follows, called *tikkun hatzot* (literally, "repair of midnight"), is understood as a time when it is easier to communicate directly with God, to experience the presence of God. It is thought of as the kindness of the night, a good time to meditate, to study Torah secrets—a time for mystical revelation.

In the next two hours we will meditate on Hebrew letters that form the name of God: *Yod Heh Vav Heh*. In Jewish mysticism, Hebrew letters are believed to have a lot of power and significance, and many meditative practices use them to uncover hidden meaning. A dozen people of differing ages, races, and religions have gathered for the meditation. Mark is a long-haired rabbinical student and a member of the congregation. Diane is a Christian with a profound interest in Judaism and an eclectic religious background. Jodi likes to call herself "goddish" rather than Jewish. Two of the dozen people are African Americans.

Goldhamer tells us a little bit about the mystical tradition of Judaism before we begin. Abraham Abulafia, a thirteenth-century mystical teacher, developed practices for meditating upon God's name and the letters of the name. Hasidism, though popularly understood today as being ultra-orthodox, represented in its pietistic eighteenth-century beginnings a radical break from the view that religious adequacy depended on scholarship. Given its populist origin, Hasidism is rich in mystical teachings.

Goldhamer is assisted by Melinda Stengel, a Catholic psychotherapist with whom he has written a book on meditation called *This Is for Everyone: Universal Principles of Healing Prayer and the Jewish Mystics*. Melinda has drawn up the sheets of paper we will be using, which contain the four letters of God's name and some directions for what to say and do.

We are sitting in a circle of chairs right next to the Ark, a curtained-off partition where the Torah, Judaism's scripture, is kept. Goldhamer asks us to look at the four letters on paper. They are not just letters, he explains: They *are* God. In mystical fashion, as we concentrate and repeat prayers in a certain order, hold and move our bodies in specified ways, we are attempting to behold God. Eyes close; hands wave. The name feels like a summons: God is name, named, namer, nameless. The aim is *devekut*—mystical cleaving to God.

The power and meaning of night is much talked about in the literature of mystics: Jewish mystics, all mystics. At this still time of night, when the mind is usually unplugged from ordinary consciousness, the atmosphere seems somehow more receptive. *Kabbalah,* the name given to the central teachings of Jewish mysticism, means "that which is received." The last meditation session produced some powerful visualizations; tonight, we simply come back to the concrete here inside Bene Shalom and a very late now—it's past two o'clock in the morning—after a feeling of somehow having been somewhere else, experiencing something nameless.

As it sweeps the Jewish community, Jewish meditation is enriching liberal Jewish worship. Deeply rooted in traditional practices, teachings, texts, and prayers, much of contemporary Jewish meditation is a rediscovery of what was always there within Judaism. For meditators, Jewish meditation offers fresh entry to thousands of years of received wisdom and practices. As much a part of life as it is a discrete practice, Jewish meditation is a contemporary, and ancient, way of keeping the name of God always before one: "I have set the Lord always before me" (Psalm 16:8). This scriptural passage offers one summary of the practice and purpose of Jewish meditation.

Constant Awareness, Continual Blessing

"A Jew is supposed to be connected all the time," says Rachmiel. "We are supposed to know God in all our ways." Rachmiel, a member of

Makom Shalom, a Jewish Renewal congregation in downtown Chicago, hosts a gathering, a *seudat shilishit* (mystical extra Sabbath meal), once a month, on the first Saturday of the month on the Jewish calendar, in his west-suburban Oak Park home. The gathering brings together people interested in meditation and study to close the Sabbath, which is a time for resting from usual work and for attending to religious and family life.

The modest, older home in this picturesque suburb where Rachmiel lives with his wife, Tamar, and their infant daughter is virtually a gallery of Judaica: pictures, posters, art, and ritual objects. A different mezuzah is nailed to the post of each door in the house. These little scrolls of paper in holders contain Judaism's essential prayer, referred to by its Hebrew name, *Sh'ma:* "Hear, O Israel: The Lord our God, the Lord is one" (Deuteronomy 6:4). Explains Rachmiel, "It reminds you that God should be everywhere."

The goal of Jewish meditation is devekut: *mystical cleaving to God. (Photo: courtesy of Elat Chayyim Jewish Spiritual Retreat Center)*

Rachmiel's gathering is timed to close the Sabbath, so people begin to gather before sundown for meditation and Torah study. A potluck—the mystical meal for this contemporary group—will conclude the evening.

Eventually, close to twenty people arrive for the gathering. Rachmiel leads us in one of the many techniques of Jewish meditation: a meditation on Hebrew letters, combining movement, breathing, and reflection about the meaning of the letters. In the Jewish mystical tradition, letters of the alphabet are understood as many-leveled building blocks for the world of words. His words open a trove of associations with the letters as we slowly move to his directions, shaping our limbs in various ways to express the letters through our bodies. In "Meditation as Our Own Jacob's Ladder" (in *Meditation from the Heart of Judaism,* Jewish Lights, 1999), Rabbi Steve Fisdel writes, "Meditating on the Hebrew alphabet taps into the primal, creative forces that underlie the entire universe."

Rachmiel's commentary multiplies meanings and associations for what we are doing. He later explains the traditional hierarchy of meaning that Jews use to study sacred text and that meditation helps us to plumb. "You can take things on various levels," he says. The first, simple level of meaning—*peshat*—is literal. What you see is what you get: for example, we wash hands to get them clean. The second level is hint *(remez):* this could mean something deeper. It invites a second, reflective look. Perhaps hand washing says something about purification. The third level is allegorical *(darash):* at this level, we are definitely being taught something. Hand washing is symbolic and meaningful, associated with a traditionally understood body of meaning. The fourth level is that of deep secrets *(sod).* This level of ultimate meaning is hidden, but is also a level of clarity. The same system for understanding deeply applies as well when studying and interpreting Torah.

Rachel, a meditation teacher and another member of the congregation, then leads us in a different meditation technique, a meditation on the "Tree of Life" of the Jewish mystical tradition. Everyone assumes a comfortable position, some lying down, some seated in chairs, and others seated on the floor with pillows. She then plays some music and helps unfold for our minds the mystical significance of the Tree of Life. She draws our attention to various parts of the body, helping us to visualize them and associate them with the kabbalistic system of ten creative energies known as the *sefirot*. The *sefirot* are associated with different points on the human body; they also link together to make a Tree of Life. Each *sefirah* is also associated with an angel, and these, too, Rachel names, linking together symbols and qualities to suggest hidden relationships.

After meditation, the group moves into earnest discussion and study of the Torah portion that is read that week, led by two people prepared to help the group see more subtleties and significance packed into ostensibly simple words. We close with a chant and prepare ourselves for eating by ritual hand washing. The simple act of washing takes on more meaning and raises awareness when it is done slowly and thoughtfully. It is a rite of purification and an occasion for a blessing. Since I don't know Hebrew, Rachmiel says the traditional blessing as I wash. A paper with Hebrew script is posted by the sink; it is another way of keeping the name of God before one, of keeping the holy intention—*kavvanah*—in the action, any action, in all actions.

"We are supposed to know God in all our ways," Rachmiel says.

It's sundown, and after *havdalah*, the ceremony distinguishing the Sabbath from the weekdays, we can turn on the lights. Rachmiel's household keeps the Sabbath strictly *(shomer Shabbas)*: no turning on lights (prohibited because it is the equivalent of the work of making a fire), no writing, no answering the telephone since it interrupts the pause and privacy of the Sabbath. Sabbath is intended to be a rest from all the activities that busy us the rest of the week. No need for a retreat: there's a day conveniently built into every week that invites rest, study, reflection, and renewal.

"The idea that you have to live in an ashram to meditate—that's *not* a Jewish thing," says Rachmiel. "We're supposed to be living in this world, shining the light, walking the path every day."

He certainly lives in the world. He is a public defender who recently spent a few months at home on paternity leave with an infant daughter. His wife, Tamar, a clinical psychologist, is beginning her study of Torah and exposure to the vast world of Jewish mystical knowledge and practice. The two met at their temple in 1998, the first time Tamar attended. They were married in 1999.

Seeking and Finding: Stories from Practitioners

Rachmiel: "We meditate for ourselves and for the world"
Rachmiel, forty-one and with just a little gray appearing in his beard, says he's been a spiritual seeker for a long time, "and only recently been a bit of a finder." He grew up in a family practicing Reform Judaism, one of the four major branches of Judaism and considered the most liberal with respect to observance of ritual practices.

"We loved pepperoni pizza and crab night," he says of his distinctly nonkosher childhood diet. As much as he loved crab—shellfish are not kosher—he adopted a kosher diet in 1997. His spiritual path was a step here, a step there. He began attending temple regularly in 1994, and he went to Israel in 1996, bringing back a *tallit* (prayer shawl) and *tefillin* (phylacteries), the latter being two small black-leather boxes containing specially prepared pieces of parchment inscribed with Torah passages. Each box is attached to a leather strap; one is to be worn on the forehead, the other wrapped on the arm and hand. Men are required to wear *tallit* and *tefillin* during morning prayers, and Rachmiel began doing that in 1996.

"That's a major step for a lot of people," he says. Despite its historic position as least traditional about ritual observances, Reform Judaism is now moving toward encouragement of the use of these and performance of other rituals. Next, Rachmiel got an Orthodox prayer book, and then he started praying three times daily (also as is traditional), got stricter about keeping the Sabbath, and began studying texts and Kabbalah in Hebrew. Recently he led services at the temple in the rabbi's absence; a friend in his meditation circle describes him as "resident Kabbalist." Rachmiel gives me a simple example of "keeping the Lord always before you": on his desk at work, he says, is a mystical explanation of the deepest levels of a line of prayer.

His job as a public defender, which he's had since 1996, fits in well with his understanding of Jewish teachings. "We know that mystically there are both accusing angels and defending angels in the Heavenly Court, and you need to have both," he explains. Rachmiel is named after his great-grandfather, and his Hebrew name means "angel of mercy."

"We meditate for ourselves and for the world," Rachmiel says. "We are not meditating *just* to clear our minds."

Michael: "Do the little things"

Tikkun olam—repair of the world—is an important responsibility for many of those involved in Jewish meditation and their rededication to a personal and meaningful practice of their religion. Michael, thirty-five, is studying at the Chicago campus of the University of Illinois for a master's degree in public health. He is interested in community nutrition and antihunger issues. When he was in Berkeley for most of the decade of the 1990s, he worked at the Berkeley Free Clinic.

In Berkeley, he also developed his meditation practice and a meaningful personal Jewish spirituality. It started with a class on the history of Kabbalah, which he took in 1991. The class practiced visualizations involving Hebrew letters, which Michael remembers vividly. First the class did some energy visualizations, and then began to work with the letters of God's name, *Yod Heh Vav Heh*.

"I put [the letters] on the walls of the old temple in Jerusalem. Each wall was a letter. What I can tell you? It was almost like I had a burning, my whole body was burning, the letters were burning," he recalls. "From that moment, I knew I had some connection I didn't understand to Judaism."

This was very different from Michael's previous experiences of his religion. He was brought up in the Reform tradition, a "holiday Jew" who went through the motions, went to Hebrew school.

"This class in San Francisco really opened me up to another path in Judaism," he says. But it took a while for him to pursue that path with consistency. He looked for more classes, and went to some services held by the Aquarian Minyan, a progressive Jewish congregation. He attended some classes led by meditation teacher Avram Davis, editor of *Meditation from the Heart of Judaism: Today's Teachers Share Their Practices, Techniques, and Faith* (Jewish Lights, 1999), in Davis's home, but "this was not the right time for me," he says. "It wasn't happening."

After a few years, though, the time was riper. In 1997 he went with a friend to the meditation center begun in Berkeley by Davis, Chochmat HaLev. Distraught over the recent breakup of a relationship, Michael was searching for something more than emotional ups and downs. He sat, meditated, and listened to Davis speak afterward. The subject was joy. He approached Davis later and told him about his current woes.

"He looks at me and says, 'Those socks you're wearing, I bet those are your favorite socks,'" Michael recalls. "He says, 'Look. It's not the big things, it's any little thing you can do for yourself to bring yourself joy. If wearing those socks makes you happy, wear those socks. Do the little things every day that bring you joy.'"

"That started me off on a path," Michael continues. "Little by little,

Avram had a lesson for me on how to live, how to live my life. I never had that in Hebrew school."

Michael now tries to remember to do the little things, such as being the first to greet other people, or remembering to send love ahead of him. Once, he was nervous about dealing with a woman from whom he needed something and who was reputed to be difficult. "I sent [love] ahead to a woman I had never met, and she was the nicest woman I ever talked to and she gave me everything I needed," he says. "You nurture kindness and you nurture yourself and you are changing the world, changing yourself in the process."

He has yet another reason to meditate: it keeps him healthy. He faces some chronic health problems and has studied a number of meditative and alternative practices for healing and health: *qi gong,* a Chinese movement practice; Taoist healing; internal organ massage. "You have to nurture all the parts of yourself for your health," Michael says.

Beyond Kabbalah: Intersections with Other Paths and Techniques

Kabbalah is one font of meditative wealth within Judaism. Still other techniques or schools—different teachers use different names—of Jewish meditation incorporate other practices for meditating and enlarging meditative awareness.

Rabbi David A. Cooper brings an interspiritual perspective, drawn from multiple religious traditions, into his teaching and writing. A prolific author and teacher who founded the Heart of Stillness Hermitage in Boulder, Colorado, Cooper has studied and practiced Buddhist and Sufi meditation in addition to exploring Jewish mysticism. In "The Promise of Jewish Meditation" (in *Meditation from the Heart of Judaism,* Jewish Lights, 1999), Cooper writes,

Judaism has to do with connecting mystically to a path that millions of people have walked for thousands of years. How that expresses itself we can debate, but Jewish meditation somehow fits into this path and guides us to it and along it. The question of how to begin a Jewish meditation practice is attached to where persons hold themselves Jewishly before they begin.

For those able to travel, Elat Chayyim, located in the town of Accord, New York, in the Catskill Mountains, is a magnet of spiritual energy. Opened in 1992, Elat Chayyim is a year-round retreat and study center attracting students and the country's leading Jewish meditation teachers. Elat Chayyim offers a two-year training program in Jewish spiritual direction and a full schedule of retreats, classes, and conferences on a variety of topics and practices. The center offers a special training program for advanced meditators and training for congregational and other spiritual leaders, as well as a variety of introductory forums.

Rabbi Jeff Roth, a cofounder of Elat Chayyim and now its spiritual director, says that beginners can enter Jewish contemplative practice through weekend, and longer, retreats. Retreats are more than silence; they include teaching, question-and-answer time, individual and group interviews, and familiar liturgical practices, including chanting. "Most retreats include a fair amount of liturgical chant, so it's not as austere and silent as some other retreats are," Roth says.

Teachers and retreats at the center may also incorporate contemplative practices from other religious traditions, including Buddhist mindfulness and Sufi prayer. "We do things with chant and movement that might look like Sufi *dhikr*, but from a Jewish liturgical point of view, the work we do is, in some ways, updating and making the Kabbalah available," he says. "We dwell less on any single particular form and are more dedicated to whatever works to bring wisdom and compassion into everyday life."

Sylvia Boorstein is a senior teacher at Elat Chayyim, where she has taught mindfulness training since 1993. She is also a founding teacher of Spirit Rock Meditation Center, a major American insight meditation center. The best-selling author of *It's Easier than You Think: The Buddhist Way to Happiness* (Harper San Francisco, 1995) and *That's Funny, You Don't Look Buddhist: On Being a Faithful Jew and a Passionate Buddhist*, Boorstein says that mindfulness, the other common term for insight meditation, is Jewish—indeed, it is the very essence of the Jewish way of life. She cites the essential Jewish prayer, the *Sh'ma*, which begins with the word "hear" or "listen." It's a call to wake up, which is also a quintessential Buddhist imperative. "The structure of the Jewish lifestyle is a call to mindful awakening," Boorstein says. "Everything about being a Jew supports being mindful."

Walking is one way of meditating. Meditation teacher Rami Shapiro notes that walking is prominent in scripture. "Abraham and Noah walk with God," Shapiro says. "In the rhythm of walking, all kinds of things can happen." (Photo: courtesy of Elat Chayyim Jewish Spiritual Retreat Center)

Jewish meditation employs many techniques and postures to bring the meditator to a direct experience of God. Meditation can involve sitting, dancing, walking, chanting, or contemplating. (Photo: courtesy of Elat Chayyim Jewish Spiritual Retreat Center)

At Metivta, a Los Angeles–based center for contemplative Judaism begun by Rabbi Jonathan Omer-Man, Rabbi Rami Shapiro, a poet and writer with twenty years' experience as a congregational rabbi, recently took over as senior rabbi. Metivta teaches meditation practices suitable for beginners, as well as intermediate and advanced techniques. An introductory meditation uses the *Sh'ma* prayer, repeating it, mantralike, and coordinating the phrases with in-breath and out-breath, always ending on the out-breath, "as if melting into the divine," Shapiro explains.

Other meditation techniques taught at Metivta use visualizations. Shapiro teaches an advanced meditation based on the Hasidic understanding of "five worlds," or five levels—body, heart, mind, soul, spirit—each of which has its own perception of reality. This meditation leads to the opening of nondualistic awareness, much like many Eastern meditation techniques.

Shapiro also likes to teach walking meditation, though it is different from the walking meditation commonly used in Buddhist insight meditation. "Walking is very Jewish," Shapiro says. "Abraham and Noah walk with God…. In the rhythm of walking, all kinds of things can happen."

"I can't teach yoga," the rabbi adds with a laugh, "but I can walk."

Love, Nothingness, Healing

Other Jewish practices, themes, and teachings are at the heart of other kinds of meditation. Some focus on *hesed* (lovingkindness) and increasing *hesed* through the practice of meditation. Some focus on the breath. Some offer insight to connections or relationships. *Ayin* meditation is another form: *ayin* means "nothingness." This kind of meditation can be compared to the Buddhist meditation that opens *shunyata*—void or emptiness—to the meditative mind. *Ayin* is a mystical notion that opens the door to liberation and egolessness. All Jewish meditation is intended to be profoundly transformative and make it easy to see and live the holy in the world.

For some practitioners, healing meditation has enriched their spiritual practice. Mark is studying healing meditation with his rabbi, Douglas Goldhamer. He is also studying to be a rabbi who will work with the deaf, as Goldhamer now does. Mark, thirty-two, remembers wanting to be a rabbi when he was eleven or twelve, but he ended up writing poetry and getting a master's degree in fine arts.

"I was the kid who liked Sunday school," he says. "I was ready for a religious high, and that didn't happen so I kind of wandered away from Judaism for a while. I was looking for this transcendent experience of some sort. I was looking for magic, maybe."

Instead, he started learning sign language, an interest that eventually grew into a goal. He learned about Goldhamer's congregation, having grown up in a nearby town. And he began studying and practicing healing meditation, partly motivated by physical difficulties with his hands stemming from overuse in signing.

Healing meditation is a good entry point for people interested in Jewish meditation, Mark says. It will introduce them to what may be unfamiliar form and technique for working with the mind. "The first step in meditation is learning how to quiet your mind," he says. "You focus on breath and do exercises to help you clear the clutter."

Mark's rabbi, Douglas Goldhamer, teaches healing meditation because it worked for him. He tells a complicated story simply.

"Twenty years ago, I was told I had an incurable disease, a blood-clotting disease, and amputation was mandated," he explains. "I found a rabbi whose meditation was healing—kabbalistic—and studied with him for a year. I began feeling, 'This is a discipline that I must embrace.' I came about studying and teaching it. It's become an essential part of my life."

Today, he says, "My limbs are normal, I'm completely healed. People think I'm a little off the wall, but...." Goldhamer is the rabbi of Bene Shalom, the only full-service synagogue for the deaf in the United States. Weekly services are signed. "I just think people should share their gifts," he says. "I think sign language and meditation both are instruments that bring me closer to God."

Goldhamer's interest in Jewish mysticism and his interest in serving the deaf community have a common thread: he believes in accessibility for all. Flowing from his experience with healing, he studies and teaches Kabbalah as a source for healing. "I feel that God should be accessible to all people. If I were a Catholic, I would be fighting for all of us to say the Mass.... In the same way, I don't think there should be a few rabbis with a claim to this esoteric wisdom."

Goldhamer has been teaching healing meditation as well as Kabbalah for a half-dozen years, and says that healing is more popular. Sometimes classes run to a hundred students, with a noticeable proportion of them Christians. "People want to be healed," he observes.

He has a grand vision for his congregation that seamlessly weaves together his interests in and practice of kabbalistic healing meditation. "My goal is that the synagogue shall become a scriptural workout center where we regularly walk hand in hand with God," he says. "We can do this through esoteric principles and achieve physical healing through religion, concomitant with our physicians."

Meditation for healing, meditation as healing, is also important to Jodi, a social worker who attended Goldhamer's midnight meditation. She makes it very clear that she doesn't want to be *labeled* Jewish, although that's the tradition in which she was brought up. She now prefers the term "goddish." "I have a little problem with labeling," she says, "because it just seems to separate people."

Jodi was raised a "holiday Jew": she attended temple twice a year, for the solemn Jewish high holy period that opens with Rosh Hashanah and closes with Yom Kippur, a day of atonement. But if the holidays were "high," they weren't particularly holy. "It was about getting nice clothes," she says. "The institutionalized religion that I grew up with did not connect me with what I experienced. It connected me with 'you get dressed up for the holidays, you say these prayers.' But I always did like the ritual aspect, the lighting of the candles and other things."

Other things also bothered her. "Death is hard in Judaism," she says. "I remember going up to my rabbi and saying, 'Is there anything after this?'"

And so religion and spirituality weren't much a part of Jodi's life as she got married and had a son, but life has a way of changing. Her home life of being a mother and volunteer unraveled when her fourteen-year marriage ended. She finished her master's degree in 2000 and began a course of bodywork therapy in order to clean her psychic attic and get clearer as she embarked on a career of helping others with their troubles. Through craniosacral therapy she experienced what she calls, in classic meditator's language, an awakening.

"I get it, I get what we're doing here, what we're supposed to be doing here, I get my own religion more," she explains. With that, she began to meditate, but not exclusively in a Jewish way. She is reading the Hindu Bhagavad Gita scripture and the Christian Gospel of Matthew about the life of Christ. She attended a series of presentations about world religions at a Unity Church in Chicago—a series in which Rachmiel spoke about Judaism.

"We're all talking about the same thing, so let's just go there," says Jodi, who is thirty-eight. "It's also love. In meditation the feeling of unconditional universal love that comes over me is just uncanny."

In her eclectic study of spirituality and healing she came to Goldhamer's book and his classes on healing meditation. "I finally found my Jewish roots through his book, so I see how I fit here," she says. Jodi regularly does healing meditation with a prayer partner who suffers from multiple sclerosis.

Now when she sees clients, she doesn't exactly see herself as just a social worker. "I'm a healer," she says. "I connected with God, some healing energy. The puzzle pieces are starting to fit together."

Michael remembers vividly a talk he heard, given by meditation teacher Avram Davis at Chochmat HaLev in Berkeley, that confirmed for him that meditation is the path, the right path, the Jewish path.

> [Avram Davis] was talking about how our natural place to sit is the seat of joy, and that's what God wants for us. To me, it's sort of like when you tune a guitar and in the middle is a natural place. The place you always fall back on is a place of joy. That was a radical concept to me: *joy*, as opposed to an obsessive place, or complaining, or life is just suffering, the world is pain and suffering. Here's a guy saying the world is actually joy. . . . Do the little things every day that bring you joy.

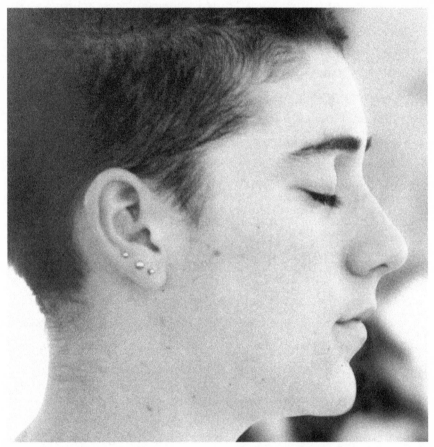

The regular practice of Jewish meditation, performed each day, helps bring the consciousness of God into every action, however insignificant. (Photo: courtesy of Elat Chayyim Jewish Spiritual Retreat Center)

Steps for Beginners

- Get going. Rabbi Jonathan Omer-Man, a leading meditation teacher and founder of the meditation center Metivta,
  emphasizes what may seem obvious, but serves as a
  reminder of the necessity for steady practice. A meditator,
  he likes to say, is someone who meditates. Nothing less
  will do.

- Omer-Man makes a second point that few meditation
  teachers advertise up front: Get used to boredom. He calls
  it "noble boredom." Experienced meditators are familiar
  with this kind of experience within a long-term practice.
  The inner journey that is meditation may not be lit by
  showering astral lights. Silence has no qualities. It is also
  difficult to maintain.

- Understand the vocabulary and teachings that Jewish
  meditation works with. People with a Jewish upbringing
  already have taken steps down the path, but Jewish meditation casts Judaism and its traditions in a new and meaningful light. Others may have to do some preliminary
  research.

- Find a community. It is the best way to support spiritual
  growth and remain plugged in to the proving ground of
  the world. The Jewish spiritual tradition is neither monastic nor renunciatory, but strongly grounded in communal
  life as the realm for the expression of spirituality. Moses
  came down from the mountain.

Many Jewish meditators use meditation as one way to renew their
entire spiritual understanding and practice of Judaism. In this sense,
meditation is indeed spiritually transformative. Observance in all areas
of life is one way of keeping the name of God before one always. In "Go
to Your Self" (in *Meditation from the Heart of Judaism*, Jewish Lights,
1999), Andrea Cohen-Kiener writes,

Jewish practices of talking, eating, waking up in the morning, dressing, praying, farming, taxing, even walking through a doorway can be described as balancing acts that let us simultaneously enjoy our physical pleasures and be mindful of God. ... *With this consciousness, our every act becomes a meditation.*

Selected Resources

Books

Boorstein, Sylvia. *Don't Just Do Something, Sit There: A Mindfulness Retreat with Sylvia Boorstein.* San Francisco: Harper San Francisco, 1996.

Cooper, David A. *The Handbook of Jewish Meditation Practices: A Guide for Enriching the Sabbath and Other Days of Your Life.* Woodstock, Vt.: Jewish Lights, 2000.

Davis, Avram, ed. *Meditation from the Heart of Judaism: Today's Teachers Share Their Practices, Techniques, and Faith.* Woodstock, Vt.: Jewish Lights, 1999.

————. *The Way of Flame: A Guide to the Forgotten Mystical Tradition of Jewish Meditation.* Woodstock, Vt.: Jewish Lights, 1999.

Dosick, Wayne. *Soul Judaism: Dancing with God into a New Era.* Woodstock, Vt.: Jewish Lights, 1999.

Frankiel, Tamar, and Judy Greenfeld. *Entering the Temple of Dreams: Jewish Prayers, Movements, and Meditations for the End of the Day.* Woodstock, Vt.: Jewish Lights, 2000.

————. *Minding the Temple of the Soul: Balancing Body, Mind, and Spirit through Traditional Jewish Prayer, Movement, and Meditation.* Woodstock, Vt.: Jewish Lights, 1997.

Gefen, Nan Fink. *Discovering Jewish Meditation: Instruction and Guidance for Learning an Ancient Spiritual Practice.* Woodstock, Vt.: Jewish Lights, 1999.

Goldhamer, Douglas, and Melinda Stengel. *This Is for Everyone: Universal Principles of Healing Prayer and the Jewish Mystics.* Burdett, N.Y.: Larson Publications, 1999.

Kamenetz, Rodger. *Stalking Elijah: Adventures with Today's Jewish Mystical Masters.* San Francisco: Harper San Francisco, 1997.

Kaplan, Aryeh. *Jewish Meditation: A Practical Guide.* New York: Schocken Books, 1985.

Kushner, Lawrence. *The Book of Letters: A Mystical Hebrew Alphabet.* Woodstock, Vt.: Jewish Lights, 1991.

———. *The Way Into Jewish Mystical Tradition.* Woodstock, Vt.: Jewish Lights, 2001.

Lew, Alan, with Sherril Jaffe. *One God Clapping: The Spiritual Path of a Zen Rabbi.* Woodstock, Vt.: Jewish Lights, 2001.

Shapiro, Rami M. *Minyan: Ten Principles for Living a Life of Integrity.* New York: Bell Tower, 1997.

Audiotapes

Cooper, David A. *The Holy Chariot.* Louisville, Colo.: Sounds True, #F062.

———. *Kabbalah Meditation.* Louisville, Colo.: Sounds True, #W268.

———. *The Mystical Kabbalah.* Louisville, Colo.: Sounds True, #F020.

Zeller, David. *The Tree of Life.* Louisville, Colo.: Sounds True, #F042.

Centers and organizations

Chochmat HaLev
1534 Prince Street
Berkeley, CA 94705
510-704-9687
www.chochmat.org

Congregation Beth Sholom
1301 Clement Street
San Francisco, CA 94188
415-221-8736
www.uscj.org/ncalif/sanfracb
www.makor-or.org

Elat Chayyim
99 Mill Hook Road
Accord, NY 12404
1-800-398-2630
www.elatchayyim.org

Metivta
2001 South Barrington Avenue, Suite 106
Los Angeles, CA 90025-5363
310-477-5370
www.metivta.org

Other sources of information

ALEPH: Alliance for Jewish Renewal
7318 Germantown Avenue
Philadelphia, PA 19119-1973
215-247-9700
www.aleph.org
(Jewish Renewal is a worldwide, transdenominational movement grounded in Judaism's mystical traditions. ALEPH has a variety of programs it offers to the public, and it organizes and nurtures communities, develops leadership, creates new liturgy and other resources, and works for social and environmental justice.)

Jewish Lights Publishing
Sunset Farm Offices
Route 4
P.O. Box 237
Woodstock, VT 05091
802-457-4000
www.jewishlights.com
(A publishing company providing books that reflect the Jewish wisdom tradition for people of all faiths, all backgrounds, particularly focusing on Jewish spirituality, mysticism, and meditation.)

8

Staying Seated:
Developing Your Practice

"The Path Is the Goal"

So you've slowed down and started meditating. Now what?

Be prepared for changes. But they may not be what you think they should be, and they may not happen when you think they should happen. That's OK. Your thinking will change, over time and with practice. Your expectations will change, loosening their grip. Your needs will change: meditation will become more and more needed. Your view of yourself will change, as the ego—the big "I" of self-awareness—gets placed in a much larger awareness, whether it be a different and relational connection with the Divine or a sense of the true nature of all things that exist.

Beginning meditators say they can notice changes in themselves: greater calmness; more clarity, whether in mental activity or personal priorities; increased patience; and a little less attachment to outcomes.

In my work on this book, I found no one, however, who reported instant enlightenment, no matter how greatly it was desired. Instant gratification is more appropriate for microwave soup than a spiritual journey.

And so the beginning meditator should also be prepared for the long road—for what Rabbi Jonathan Omer-Man compellingly terms "noble boredom"—and for resistance, inertia, and distraction.

Distractions can be as fleeting as a quickly passing thought, as weighty as significant bad news, as repugnant as unpleasant personal revelations, or as insidious as the slow acid drip of doubt on faith. Like demons, questions soon enough plague the meditator: *Why am I just sitting here? What good is this doing? What difference does this make?*

It *does* make a difference. It especially makes a difference during times of personal or global tumult, times when it is very, very hard to *just* sit. The sages and saints of the spiritual wisdom traditions have known that the surest way to get past something is to go all the way *into* and *through* it in order to emerge *beyond* it. Meditators come to learn this through their accumulated experience.

Ebb is linked to flow; meditators sometimes take time off from practice. Yet ultimately you have to do the work, they say. No one else can do it for you. Resistance is just part of the process. "The path is the goal," Tibetan Buddhist teacher Chogyam Trungpa emphatically and eloquently said. Sometimes the path is rocky, sometimes the path is smooth. That is the true nature of any path.

So keep moving. Keep sitting. Meditate when thoughts are flying like bats out of a cave, when the mind pursues a passing thought like a child chasing a beautiful butterfly. Meditate when there are cries of mourning; the practice deepens compassion and affords greater awareness of the Unity that manifests itself in the diversity that comes and goes. Meditate when you don't want to, even if only a little.

Each experience of meditation is one more opportunity for enlightenment, for insight, for compassion, for union, for growth. In the beginner's mind there are many such possibilities, many such opportunities.

Keep beginner's mind.

To help you keep that mind, here are a few additional resources.

Additional Resources for New Meditators

Books

Boorstein, Sylvia. *That's Funny, You Don't Look Buddhist: On Being a Faithful Jew and a Passionate Buddhist.* San Francisco: Harper San Francisco, 1998.

Cooper, David A. *A Heart of Stillness: A Complete Guide to Learning the Art of Meditation.* Woodstock, Vt.: SkyLight Paths, 1999.

Cooper, David A. *Three Gates to Meditation Practice: A Personal Journey into Sufism, Buddhism, and Judaism.* Woodstock, Vt.: SkyLight Paths, 2000.

Dass, Ram. *Journey of Awakening: A Meditator's Guidebook.* New York: Bantam, 1990.

Goleman, Daniel. *The Meditative Mind: The Varieties of Meditative Experience.* New York: Tarcher/Putnam, 1988.

Kamenetz, Rodger. *The Jew in the Lotus.* New York: HarperCollins, 1995.

Krishnamurti, J. *This Light in Oneself: True Meditation.* Boston: Shambhala, 1999.

Morreale, Don. *The Complete Guide to Buddhist America.* Boston: Shambhala, 1998.

Smith, Huston. *The World's Religions.* San Francisco: Harper San Francisco, 1991.

Smith, Jean, ed. *Breath Sweeps Mind: A First Guide to Meditation Practice.* New York: Riverhead, 1998.

Teasdale, Wayne. *The Mystic Heart: Discovering a Universal Spirituality in the World's Religions.* Novato, Calif.: New World Library, 1999.

Centers and Organizations

Lama Foundation
505-758-8622
505-586-1269
www.lamafoundation.org
(An intentional spiritual community and educational center in northern New Mexico, teaching a diversity of practices from many spiritual traditions.)

Shem Center for Interfaith Spirituality
708 North Harvey Avenue
Oak Park, IL 60302-1742
708-848-095
http://members.aol.com/SHEMCenter
(A center where the prayer, meditation, rituals, and wisdom of the peoples of the world can be experienced and reflected upon.)

Internet Sites

- www.rsl.ukans.edu/~pkanagar/meditation—The nonsectarian home page of the University of Kansas Meditation Club, with great links and resources.

Other Sources of Information

Sounds True
P.O. Box 8010
Boulder, CO 80306-8010
800-333-9185
www.soundstrue.com
(An audio, video, and music publishing company offering more than five hundred titles about spiritual traditions, meditation, psychology, creativity, health and healing, self-discovery, relationships, and more.)

Tricycle: The Buddhist Review
92 Vandam Street
New York, NY 10013
212-645-1143
www.tricycle.com
(A nonprofit quarterly magazine containing articles, resources, and information about Buddhism.)

Glossary

Note: square brackets [] designate the original language of the term; braces {} designate the tradition(s) in which the term is used.

Asana [Sanskrit] {Hindu}: Pose, posture in hatha yoga exercises.

Bodhisattva [Sanskrit] {Buddhist}: "Enlightenment being"; bodhisattvas are understood to be perfect beings—some earthly, some transcendent—who help other beings attain enlightenment.

Brahman [Sanskrit] {Hindu}: God, understood as formless, infinite, and absolute.

Chakra [Sanskrit] {Hindu, Buddhist, Sufi}: "Wheel"; *chakra*s are centers of subtle energy, which Eastern thought understands as being present in key places in the body.

Dharma [Sanskrit; in Pali, *dhamma*] {Hindu, Buddhist}: In Hinduism, truth or religious duty; in Buddhism, phenomenon; teaching of the Buddha.

Dhikr [Arabic] {Sufi}: Practice of the "remembrance of God."

Dhyana [Sanskrit] {Hindu}: Meditation, in the sense of attention flowing in an unbroken stream toward an object of meditation.

Dokusan [Japanese] {Buddhist}: Private meeting of Zen teacher and student.

Dukkha [Pali; in Sanskrit, *duhkha*] {Buddhist}: Suffering, dissatisfaction, that which is conditioned.

Enneagram: [Greek] {Sufi, Christian, others}: System of personality types used in many mystical traditions, including Sufi and Catholic.

Fana [Arabic] {Sufi}: Annihilation of self or ego.

Gomden [Tibetan] {Buddhist}: Square meditation cushion used by followers of Chogyam Trungpa.

Guru [Sanskrit] {Hindu, Buddhist}: Accomplished teacher.

Hadith (plural, ahadith) [Arabic] {Sufi}: Saying, teaching, or action of the Prophet Muhammad used as a guideline for Muslim behavior.

Kabbalah [Hebrew] {Jewish}: "The received"; esoteric teachings of Judaism.

Kasa [Korean; Japanese, *rakusu*] {Buddhist}: Biblike outer robe worn by Zen Buddhist practitioner.

Koan [Japanese; Korean, *kong-an*] {Buddhist}: A conundrum or paradox given to a Zen student to confound rational thought and train the mind in nondualistic thinking.

Kyosaku [Japanese] {Buddhist}: "Wake-up stick" used in Zen Buddhist meditation.

Lama [Tibetan] {Buddhist}: "Superior one"; spiritual teacher, and also a polite title for all Tibetan monks.

Lectio divina [Latin] {Christian}: "Divine reading"; a process of attending to and contemplating scripture as a means for deepening a relationship with God. *Lectio divina* begins with reading a small portion of scripture in order to approach God through the vehicle of sacred text. *Lectio divina* is intended to lead to reflection, prayer, and, ultimately, contemplative communion with God.

Mahayana [Sanskrit] {Buddhist}: "Great vehicle"; applied to the body of Buddhist teachings and practices that emphasizes the saving of all sentient beings. It is one of three major branches of Buddhism, along with Theravada and Vajrayana Buddhism, and it flourishes today in India, China, Japan, Korea, Europe, and North

America. (Zen is a school of Buddhism in the Mahayana tradition.)

Mandala [Sanskrit] {Hindu, Buddhist}: "Circle"; symbol of diverse cosmic forces and their underlying order.

Mantra [Sanskrit] {Hindu, Buddhist}: A sacred syllable, word, or phrase used for chanting or meditation.

Metta [Pali] {Buddhist}: Kindness.

Moksha [Sanskrit] {Hindu}: Liberation.

Niyama [Sanskrit] {Hindu}: Observance; practice or behavior to be followed.

Pir [Persian]; {Sufi}: Elder; title for the spiritual head of a Sufi order.

Prana [Sanskrit] {Hindu}: Vital energy; equated in the West with breath.

Rakusu [Japanese; Korean, *Kasa*] {Buddhist}: Biblike outer robe worn by Zen Buddhist practitioner.

Rinpoche [Tibetan] {Buddhist}: "Jewel" or "precious one"; honorific title for Tibetan teacher.

Roshi [Japanese] {Buddhist}: Respected or senior teacher in Zen.

Samadhi [Sanskrit] {Hindu, Buddhist}: Absorption, merging in union with the Divine or with the object of meditation; a nondualistic state of consciousness.

Sangha [Sanskrit] {Buddhist}: Strictly, monastic community; often used in insight/*vipassana* simply to designate community.

Satori [Japanese] {Buddhist}: Sudden enlightenment or awakening in Zen.

Sefirot [Hebrew] {Jewish}: System of spiritual energy centers in human body; taught in Jewish mysticism.

Seiza [Japanese] {Buddhist}: Position of sitting while kneeling; also used for bench employed in this position.

Sensei [Japanese] {Buddhist}: Title of respect given to Zen teacher.

Sesshin [Japanese] {Buddhist}: Period of intensive practice; retreat.

Shariah [Arabic] {Sufi}: Islamic sacred law.

Shaykh [Arabic] {Sufi}: Elder; title for a Sufi teacher.

Swami [Sanskrit] {Hindu}: Master; title used for Hindu monks.

Tantrism [Sanskrit] {Hindu, Buddhist}: An esoteric vehicle to achieving enlightenment, using meditation, tantras (texts of special teachings), mandalas, mantras, and *mudra*s (symbolic gestures). Tantrism channels mental, physical, and emotional energies through discipline and ritual action to expedite enlightenment.

Theravada [Sanskrit] {Buddhist}: "Way of the elders"; applied to the body of Buddhist teachings and practices that center around individual liberation. It is one of three major branches of Buddhism, along with Mahayana and Vajrayana Buddhism, and it flourishes today in Thailand, Myanmar (Burma), Cambodia, Laos, Sri Lanka, Europe, and North America. It regards itself as closest to the "original" Buddhism taught by the Buddha himself. (Theravada Buddhism is sometimes referred to as *Hinayana*, or "lesser vehicle, a term Theravadans regard as derogatory.")

Vajrayana [Sanskrit] {Buddhist}: "Diamond vehicle"; applied to the body of Tibetan Buddhist teachings and practices. Although it is a form of Mahayana Buddhism, it is often viewed as a separate "vehicle," one of three major branches of Buddhism along with Theravada and Mahayana Buddhism. A distinguishing feature is its use of tantra (see above)—esoteric teachings—to attain enlightenment.

Veda [Sanskrit] {Hindu}: Sacred scripture of Hinduism.

Vipassana [Pali; Sanskrit, *vipashyana*] {Buddhist}: Insight; commonly applied to a form of meditation most prominent in Theravada Buddhism.

Yama [Sanskrit] {Hindu}: Restraint; practice or behavior to be avoided.

Yana [Sanskrit] {Buddhist}: Path or vehicle; used as suffix describing different Buddhist traditions or schools—e.g., Mahayana, Vajrayana.

Yoga [Sanskrit] {Hindu}: Union or yoke; used to describe a set of spiritual practices leading to union with the Divine.

Zabuton [Japanese] {Buddhist}: Mat used in meditation, placed underneath *zafu*.

Zafu [Japanese] {Buddhist}: Round meditation cushion.

Zazen [Japanese] {Buddhist}: "Just sitting"; absorption in meditation.

Zendo [Japanese] {Buddhist}: Meditation room or place.

Printed in the USA
CPSIA information can be obtained
at www.ICGtesting.com
JSHW022335140824
68134JS00019B/1504